Sarojini Naidu

Sarojini Naidu

Her Way With Words

Edited and Introduced by
Mushirul Hasan

NIYOGI
BOOKS

This book is a collaborative effort between the
NATIONAL ARCHIVES OF INDIA and NIYOGI BOOKS

Published by
NIYOGI BOOKS
D-78, Okhla Industrial Area, Phase-I
New Delhi-110 020, INDIA
Tel: 91-11-26816301, 49327000
Fax: 91-11-26810483, 26813830
email: niyogibooks@gmail.com
website: www.niyogibooks.com

Editor: Mushirul Hasan
Photographs: Nehru Memorial Museum & Library, New Delhi

ISBN: 978-93-81523-43-8
Publication: 2012

Design: Shashi Bhushan Prasad/Niyogi Books

Printed at: Niyogi Offset Pvt. Ltd., New Delhi, India

Front cover: Portrait of Sarojini Naidu c.1920s (Nehru Memorial Museum & Library, New Delhi).

Contents

Editor's Note

With lute in our hands ever singing we roam,

All men our kindred, the world is our own.

From "Wandering Singers", in *The Golden Threshold* (1905)

The woman who wrote these lines was none other than Sarojini Naidu (née Chattopadhyaya), the poet-patriot born on 13 February 1897. Her father was an educationist and her mother, an accomplished poet. She was one of the most outstanding women of her time. Her contemporaries remember vividly the crowds which flocked to hear her speak. As a public figure and a poet, few women have been so effective. She began to compose poems at a young age. Slowly and steadily, no doubt, but quite definitely, she excelled in many fields.

Arnold Toynbee observed: 'What we mean by greatness, of any degree, in a human being is, I should say, the power, in some measure and in some field, to move other human beings.' Sarojini Naidu did just that. In Attia Hosain's enchanting novel, *Sunlight on a Broken Column*, she is described as 'a leader in the new social world. She won people with her charm, intrigued them with her calculated attack on conventions, titillated them with her cynical coquetry and impressed them with her hospitality and her wealth. She had become a patroness of the arts, a benefactress of impecunious writers and artists, [and] a collector of ancient works of art and young lovers.'[1]

This book is based exclusively on the resources available at the National Archives of India, New Delhi. The photographs are from the Nehru Memorial Museum & Library in New Delhi. This is the first

1. Attia Hossain. *Sunlight on a Broken Column*. (New Delhi, 2009), p. 175.

step towards making some of our personal collections available to the general reader.

The existing literature on Sarojini Naidu is rather limited. Besides letters compiled by Makarand Paranjape, Tara Ali Baig, a close friend and admirer wrote about her. Her book in the 'Builders of Modern India' series is well researched. Hasi Banerjee and V.S. Naravane have analysed the *Bulbul-i Hind*'s poetry. Padmini Sengupta's full-length biography, *Sarojini Naidu: A Biography* merits serious attention. Other works are by P.E. Dustoor and Sarla Jag Mohan. I have also made use of the writings of Jawaharlal Nehru, Vijaya Lakshmi Pandit, Krishna Nehru Hutheesingh, M.R.A. Baig, the Sandhurst-educated diplomat, and the renowned jurist, M.C. Chagla. The diaries of Asaf Ali, the Delhi lawyer, that I recently came across also proved to be an important source for Sarojini's stay in London.

My introduction focuses on Sarojini Naidu's public role, because she was politically-minded. Mine is a historian's tribute to her generosity; her mental and moral integrity; her devotion to duty; her untiring efforts to preserve India's pluralism; her display of literary brilliance; and, above all, her ability to live with honesty, dignity, and patriotic endeavour with international cooperation.

Mushirul Hasan
Director-General, National Archives of India
New Delhi, May 2012

Introduction
Sarojini Naidu: A Magnificence of Spirit

> The great Father of the Nation and this great woman (Sarojini Naidu) have shaped our national movement so powerfully, not so much on the direct political plane, although she was active there and adequately functioned, but in those invisible planes which are so very important, because they shape the nation's character; because they mould ultimately its mental and aesthetic and artistic outlook; and without that mental, moral, aesthetic and artistic outlook, any success that we may gain may well be an empty success; because, after all, we seek freedom not merely because it is good in itself, but to achieve something else. We seek freedom to achieve a good life for our people.[2]

The histories of the Indian nationalist movement cannot be written without mentioning the Anand Bhawan in Allahabad, the Darus-Salam in Delhi, and the Golden Threshold in Hyderabad, once a princely state. These houses provide a glimpse into the lives of some prominent persons and their families, and obliterate, strictly speaking, the public-private distinction. I endeavour to bring them into the historian's domain and, in the process, construct aspects of Sarojini Naidu's role in public life.

Anand Bhawan

Allahabad means 'City of God.' This is a holy city, where the confluence of the Ganga and the Yamuna takes place. Pilgrims to this sacred city come from everywhere, especially during the great Kumbh Mela, held

2. Mushirul Hasan (ed.), *Nehru's India: Select Speeches* (New Delhi, 2007), p. 269.

every twelve years. Every year smaller pilgrims attend the Magh Mela. They plod patiently along in the heat and dust, but are supported and sustained by an unwavering faith and belief. They are serenely content at the prospect of being cleansed from every vestige of sin by those holy waters.

Mark Twain described Allahabad—the British section—in the following words:

> It is a town of wide avenues and noble distances, and is comely and alluring, and full of suggestions of comfort and leisure, and of the serenity which a good conscience buttressed by a sufficient bank account gives. The bungalows stand well back in the seclusion and privacy of large enclosed compounds (private grounds, as we should say) and in the shade and shelter of trees. Even the photographer and the prosperous merchant ply their industries in the elegant reserve of big compounds, and the citizens drive in there upon their business occasions. And not in cabs—no; in the Indian cities cabs are for the drifting stranger; all the white citizens have private carriages; and each carriage has a flock of white-turbaned footmen and drivers all over it.

Near Bharadwaj Ashram (in ancient days the site of a university) is a place where once Rama and Bharat met when the Lord returned from exile. Here stands the Anand Bhawan (Abode of Happiness). When Jawaharlal Nehru was ten years old, his father Motilal Nehru, who had a full, strenuous and happy life as a lawyer, had purchased this large house with a huge garden and big verandas all around. One part of the garden had a summer-house and a tennis court. Inside the summer-house was Shiva's image mounted high on large stones, which were placed one on top of the other to make it look like a miniature mountain.[3] From Shiva's head a tiny stream trickled down into the pool at the foot of it. Anand Bhawan, wrote Vijaya Lakshmi (later,

3. Krishna Nehru Hutheesing, *With No Regrets* (London, 1944), p. 7.

Pandit), bustled with activity. Guests associated the sound of laughter with the house.[4]

To Jawaharlal, Anand Bhawan was far more than a structure of brick and concrete, more than a private possession: it was connected intimately with the freedom struggle, and within its walls great events occurred. After the first arrest of father and son in December 1921, many more family members went to gaol. For this, Sarojini Naidu admired the Nehrus. 'Across the landscape of this moving family,' wrote Sarojini Naidu, 'fall the brighter lights and the half lights, the dimmer and the deeper shadows inseparable from human destiny.' Motilal was 'Papaji'; Kamala Nehru, 'mammaji'; and Krishna Nehru, 'Betti'. On the occasion of Vijaya Lakshmi Pandit's marriage, the *Bulbul-i Hind* congratulated her: 'You are bringing as your share in that comradeship some wonderful personal gifts, enhanced by all the richness and nobility of tradition that belong to your family, as the integral part of the existing traditions, ideals and achievements which are an example and an inspiration to the nation.'[5]

In less happier times, Sarojini Naidu bore the hardships during the Home Rule movement and Rowlatt Satyagraha with much stoicism and humour. Once seen, she couldn't be forgotten because of her verbal ingenuity and the gift of electrifying audiences by her powerful oratory. Her exuberance was such that she'd put all her strength into whatever she said. Her technique, combined with her poetic nature, made her performance remarkable. She didn't prepare speeches. To speak was as easy for her as it was for a fish to swim. Halide Edip, the Turkish novelist and feminist political leader, described:

> She began in a low tone and used restrained imagery and everyday words. The tone rose gradually, adjectives became more and more colourful, and she ended on a brilliant climax. There was no hesitation in finding the words, or in constructing them into longish sentences. Her body rose with her edifice of words and images; so that, curiously enough, the short

4. Vijaya Lakshmi Pandit, *The Scope of Happiness* (New Delhi, 1979), pp. 42-43.
5. Ibid., p. 104.

> woman who had begun the speech became taller and taller as she reached the end. The fact that Sarojini actually stands on her toes at the end has nothing to do with it; that upward rise of the body is really parallel to an inward rise....it is psychological rather than physical. Without remembering what she said I confess that I was as strongly moved as the youthful audience.[6]

Sarojini Naidu found a haven in the home of kind and congenial friends like Motilal Nehru. An outspoken opponent of religious rituals and superstitions, he didn't harp on trifles and eschewed religious controversies. Sarojini Naidu shared his modern sensibilities and his spacious and unprejudiced outlook on the past and present. Indeed, they combined to add a cosmopolitan element to the Congress activities. They were both faithful to their wider political interests and were moved and uplifted by M.K. Gandhi's rise to power. Even if some differences cropped up and a shift in political outlook took place, their vigour was unabated to the end. What is more, both strove for dignity in public life. M.R.A Baig's abiding impression of the patriarch of the Nehru household is of 'an imperious Roman Senator in a snow-white toga presiding like a patriarch at a table..... His impact on Baig 'remains the greatest of the great.'[7]

Sarojini Naidu's speeches and actions inspired the Nehrus, and they grew more and more to admire her and to think of her as a rich and rare being. In 1917, Jawaharlal was moved by her speeches: 'it was all nationalism and patriotism.'[8] She exhibited, in a high degree, the perceptiveness of a poet and its corollary, the fine sense of humour and irony. The Indian bourgeoisie was, in many cases, Western through and through; Sarojini Naidu was no different. But Jawaharlal, who waited for years for his 'discovery' of India to take place, respected her adaptation to and acceptance of Indian traditions. She was, at any rate, quite free from all pretentiousness and snobbery.

---

6. Halide Edip, *Inside India*. Introduced and edited by Mushirul Hasan (New Delhi, 2000)
7. M.R.A. Baig, *In Different Saddles* (New Delhi, 1967), p. 66.
8. Jawaharlal Nehru, *An Autobiography* (London, 1936), p. 35.

Sarojini Naidu and Jawaharlal were free from the entanglements of prejudice and convention. This trait in their worldview lingered long in the thoughts of their friends and companions. When they came to political affairs, they were on each other's side—'the invincible faith of one's spirit kindles the flame of another in radiance that illumines the world'. Jawaharlal led and Sarojini followed. Her almost wayward impatience sometimes amused him, but he was impressed by her intellectual serenity in a crisis. She, in turn, had an abiding faith in his 'incorruptible sincerity and passion for liberty'.[9] Once, she reminded him that 'liberty is the ultimate crown of all your sacrifice', and assured him that 'you will not walk alone.'[10] On his fiftieth birthday, she expected him to transmute sorrow, suffering, sacrifice, anguish and strife 'into the very substance of ecstasy and victory—and freedom.' She described Jawaharlal as 'a man of destiny born to be alone in the midst of crowds, deeply loved and but little understood ...'[11]

Jawaharlal's sisters, nieces and daughter were bright and attractive; their mind was occupied upon what they considered to be the fundamental issues facing the nation. Sarojini Naidu's scintillating wit, and her spontaneous, useful, and happy life inspired them. They noticed how she turned everything into a festival with her irrepressible vivacity and *joie de vivre*, how music flowed from her lips, as it did from her pen. When Viyaya Lakshmi's husband, the barrister Ranjit Sitaram Pandit died on 14 January 1944, Sarojini Naidu's daughter rushed to console her. 'How I welcomed their coming,' she recalled.[12] And, on Diwali that year, she blessed Rajiv Gandhi:

> For, my little great-nephew, you inherit a famous ancestry and a high tradition. You are in fact yourself the lamp of life for your household ... In a free India which will be you ... you will achieve a splendid manhood and be a leader among those who dedicate their talents, their time, their

9. Sarojini Naidu to Jawaharlal Nehru, 29 September 1929, *A Bunch of Old Letters*, p. 75.
10. Ibid., 13 November 1937, p. 255.
11. Ibid., Diwali 1939, p. 407.
12. Vijaya Lakshmi Pandit, *The Scope of Happiness*, (New Delhi, 1979) p. 177.

> hope and faith and service to the redeeming of humanity from evil.[13]

Nayantara Sahgal writes in *Prison and Chocolate Cake*: 'Mother and daughter extolled her charm and her kind-hearted, friendly, and generous disposition. One can see her talking with a sort of vehemence at the All Indian Congress Committee meeting; one can see her gesticulating wildly in a public meeting; or one could see her sitting next to Gandhi during one of his many fasts.'[14] We know that Gandhi was sustained to the end by his devoted wife, his disciples, and by Sarojini Naidu who were both friends and disciples. Krishna Nehru Hutheesing was, likewise, inspired by her example:

> It was here that I met Virendra Chattopadhyaya, Sarojini Naidu's brother, for the first time. He was popularly known as Uncle Chatto. An exile for a great many years from his motherland, having wandered alone from one country to another without a home or financial means, he lived a hand-to-mouth existence. He had not become embittered as many might have done and did become. On the contrary, he always had a smile on his face and a word of good cheer for everybody. He was clever, gentle, charming and one of the most lovable characters I have ever met. I became very fond of him as he did of me, and the more I saw of him the more my respect and admiration for him increased. Even when stark hunger faced him round the corner he never lost courage. Many a time when all he had for his lunch was a couple of apples, he would insist on sharing it with some poor Indian student who was also hard up. When we went to Berlin in October 1927, we met Chatto again and saw a great deal of him. We had all become fond of him and he in turn gave us all his affection. Perhaps it was because after many years he had met some

13 Sarojini Naidu to Rajiv Gandhi, 16 October1944, Makarand Paranjape (ed.), *Sarojini Naidu: Selected Letters 1890s to 1940s* (Delhi, 1996), pp. 313-14.
14. Nayantara Sahgal, *Prison and Chocolate Cake* (New Delhi, 1997)

> people who gave him the feeling of being one of their family and not an outcast.[15]

The Golden Threshold

Hyderabad, a historic city, is enveloped in a cloud of gold, sprinkled with mauve and orange. 'What a magnificent scene', wrote a French traveller in 1937, as he witnessed the minarets soar into the magic of the sky and the white houses and terraces tinted with the ever changing hues of the sunset. One minute they were rose, then they became mauve, afterwards, a red-orange halo enriched the entire city. Some minutes later, the traveller was among the crowd: noise, music, fez, an odour of musk, camels with their proud heads held high ... Thousands of lights twinkle out.[16]

The Golden Threshold rang with laughter. It was a spacious bungalow with a walled-in compound. It had a lovely garden with fully-grown trees. Wherever Sarojini Naidu was, that was her kingdom. She loved a beautifully appointed home, rich food, beautiful clothes and jewels and a house filled with people involved with stirring events. It was an authentic 'salon' like those of Mme de Stael and Europe's other famous intellectual hostesses. Margaret Cousins commented: 'One can speculate romantically about her last incarnation, and dream of her as the bright and shining star of some brilliant salon at the height of France's glory.'[17]

'Why don't you too go on strike and hide here?', she once suggested to Jawaharlal. Although the large and extended family didn't live under the same roof, the Naidus believed that they were brought into the world in order to be happy. On 11 May 1925, Jawaharlal listened to the sun-birds and honey-birds making music in the garden among the flowering gul mohars and scarlet roses.[18] In July 1939, he and his sister Krishna lunched at the Golden Threshold.[19] Jawaharlal was drawn to her daughter as well; in later years, his sisters wanted

15. Krishna Nehru Hutheesing, *With No Regrets*, (London, 1944) pp. 40-41.
16. Louis Revel, *The Fragrance of India* (Bombay, 1946), p, 189.
17. Quoted in V.S. Naravane, *Sarojini Naidu*, p. 143.
18. Jawaharlal Nehru (ed.), *A Bunch of Old Letters*, p. 42.
19. Krishna Nehru Hutheesing, *With No Regrets*, (London, 1944) p. 135.

him married to Padmaja. Virendranath, Sarojini's brother, influenced him as well.[20]

Others, too, enjoyed the hospitality of the Naidus. The room would overflow with artists, writers, political workers, friends to the accompaniment of endless trays of coffee and cold drinks and gusts of laughter. Her charm and vivacity was such that no one had the time for anyone but her—Mohamed Ali, who acted as the Supreme Helmsman steering the Khilafat ship in an uncertain direction; Shuaib Qureshi, his son-in-law; Jamini Roy, the painter; Beverley Nichols, whose book, *Verdict on India,* created widespread indignation in India; the writer, M.R.A. Baig and his wife Tara Ali Baig, Asaf Ali, M.C. Chagla and others. Here, the host would sit cross-legged on a divan and talk with a brilliance that would remind one of her visitors of 'Lady Oxford at her best, in the old Bedford Square days, when yellow tulips were two shillings a dozen and sherry was just drink, and not an Event.'[21]Tara Ali Baig, writes:

> Brilliant, sensitive, compassionate, passionate, she led even an old misogynist like Somerset Maugham to say after meeting her at dinner, on our terrace overlooking the sea in Bombay, "Never have I met a more extraordinary woman!" The summer stars had been alight and Sarojini's chuckles and wit had enlivened the flow of talk that went on till the early hours of the morning. Like many of our people, she combined a curious mixture of sophistication and a love of the good things of life, yet had no problem whatsoever living like a peasant when she was a political detainee. Wherever she was, she brought with her that radiance of an unquenchable love of life and was always the scintillating centre of any gathering.[22]

'The Naidus stood out in every society. They exemplified the current movements in thought—from Raja Rammohun Roy's Brahmo ideology to communism and revolutionary nationalism. For the people of India,

---

20. B.N. Pandey, *Nehru* (London, p. 118
21. Beverley Nichols, *Verdict on India* (London, 1944), p. 150.
22. Tara Ali Baig, *Portrait of an Era* (Delhi, 1989, 2nd impression), p. 36.

national salvation lay in renouncing their imperial rule. Ideas of the Hindutva variety seemed to them to be grotesque. They had, in a sense, imbibed the spirit of enlightenment. Harindranath Chattopadhyaya showed the face of a poet; he wedded Kamaladevi Chattopadhyaya, Gandhi's follower and founder of the All India Women's Conference.

The revolutionary fervour wasn't lacking either. Virendranath Chattopadhyaya (Chatto), the eldest son of Aghornath, relinquished the unedifying middle-class way of life and engaged in revolutionary propaganda in London, Paris and Berlin. Founder of the Indian Committee of National Independence in 1915, he worked closely with V.D. Savarkar and Mme Bhikaji Rustom K.R. Cama;[23] In 1933, J.C. Naidu, Sarojini Naidu's son, was arrested along with A.C. Nambiar. Revolutionaries like him were brave and courageous, but the disillusioning experience of some of them demonstrated many things, including the vast and extensive intelligence network which curbed the spread of revolutionary propaganda.

Darus-Salam

Daryaganj is Delhi's original cantonment. After 1803, a native regiment of the Delhi garrison was stationed here, after which it was shifted to the Ridge area. The British Daryaganj Cantonment was one of the earliest establishments in Old Delhi. East of Daryaganj was the Yamuna River. Nearby lived Dr Mukhtar Ahmad Ansari, who had moved from Mori Gate in the old city to this area in 1925. He lived more than anyone in the 1920s to give a much-needed sense of the value of swaraj. Joseph Conrad (1857-1924)—born and bred in Poland—wrote in his preface to *A Personal Record* (1912): 'Those who read me, know my conviction that the world, the temporal world, rests on a few very simple ideas; so simple that they may be as old as the hills. It rests notably, among others, on the idea of Fidelity.' This governing idea of fidelity, of faith-keeping between man and man, was the mainspring of Ansari's life. Beneath his seriousness he was ardent and affectionate. Sarojini Naidu

23. For his role and his tension with the Congress, Milton Israel, *Communications and Power: Propaganda and the Press in the Indian Nationalist struggle, 1920-1947* (Delhi, 1994), pp. 262-63.

and others thought, that he was sincere, kind, warm-hearted, and quite innocent of guile.

Once, Darus-Salam (Abode of Islam) used to be a landmark, not far from Juma Masjid, the great mosque built by Shahjahan. Ansari hosted Indians and guests from Britain, Turkey and Egypt. Halide Edip, whom he first met as the leader of the Indian Medical Mission to Constantinople in 1912, stayed here for two months in 1935. She dug deep into Delhi's intellectual history, with a deep understanding of the circumstances in which changes occurred from time to time, describing Darus-Salam as 'an historical place where the ancient, the medieval, and the modern came together: the ideas and aspirations of divergent personalities meet, coalesce, and the personalities disperse to set in motion new trends elsewhere. In the free India of the future, that house will be one of the prinipal landmarks in the making'.[24] Her very personal narrative is closely woven into the fabric of the family history of the Ansaris. Dr Ansari himself had done much to maintain the right atmosphere.

'What news, Akka (older sister)?' Dr. Ansari would ask in the evenings, when Sarojini Naidu returned to Darus-Salam from her social activities. (A considerable number of Congress leaders called her Akka, or sister). Darus-Salam was her first home, and Ansari and his adopted daughter, Zohra, played hosts to her. She could draw on deeper and spacious reservoirs of her studies in Cambridge in the course of her conversations with the Ansaris. Comfortably seated near the little fountain in the middle of the house, they discussed poetry, Delhi's monuments and the vision of a liberal and secular society, the best of the legacies to their era, and above all, the lamentable breakdown of the Hindu-Muslim alliance after the Khilafat and Non-cooperation excitement. Invariably, they'd resolve to serve Mohandas Karamchand Gandhi and give him the strength to pursue his mission. They were neither timid nor cautious in expressing their sentiment.

Halide Edip and Sarojini Naidu had met in New York on a lecture tour, and again in England. The Turkish author stood out among the speakers as a woman of great ability, lucidity, and power, reported

24. Halide Edip, *Inside India*. Introduced and edited by Mushirul Hasan (New Delhi, 2000) p.15

Sarojini Naidu to her daughter Leilamani... Years later, Edip described her infinite variety of moods: 'When you were thinking her rather cruel, you found her suddenly as tender, as kind, as any woman could be. When you thought her nationalism was expressing itself in somewhat narrow or aggressive terms, you found a universality of spirit, a comprehension of humanity, which led you to think of her as a true citizen of the world.'[25] Jawaharlal Nehru's description matched this one. 'She was,' he said, 'like cool running water, soothing and uplifting and bringing down the passion of her politics to the cooler levels of human being. So it is difficult for one to speak about her except that one realises that here was a magnificence of spirit and it is gone.'[26]

In the mornings, Halide Edip found Sarojini Naidu basking in the sun with her long hair down her back. There was always a small table before her, with a pile of books and papers on it. She glanced through them, scribbled on a pad, talking all the while to the people. She created an atmosphere of freedom in which her guests could talk to each other; and she managed to do it with a sovereign grace, in the manner of a queen holding a court. She was no longer the satirist, but the humorist measuring the relative value of things. She'd allow nothing to go so deep as to spoil her somewhat lazy enjoyment of the sun. 'If, the night before', wrote Halide Edip, 'she had been a destructive goddess, eating her fellow-gods and goddesses, in the morning she was a serene majesty, who did not care to assert her rule at the cost of others.'

Sarojini Naidu would come back late in the evenings to Darus-Salam. She would join round the fire, throw herself into a chair, shed her slippers, and warm her bare toes. She seemed satisfied, her coffee-coloured eyes sparkling from under heavy lids. She talked, gesticulating—with her expressive brown arms. 'Scene after scene,' Halide Edip continued,

> She enfolded from the lives of the great of India. She throbbed with the fearful intellect of a futurist artist, who will wickedly, though unwittingly, distort and colour men and events to suit a fancy or whim. I do not think she deliberately meant to be

25. Ibid., p. 26
26 Mushirul Hasan (ed.) *Nehru's India: Select Speeches* (New Delhi, 2010) pp. 267-69

> untruthful: it was nothing but a powerful sense of caricature. I thought she lacked a sense of humour those evenings; for humour tones down, while she exaggerated. Further, humorous people have an inner submission to events; but, as the man in Chicago had said, she had not the slightest tendency to submissiveness. On the contrary she had the sort of personality which demanded submission from others.[27]

The Road to Destiny[28]

Aghornath Chattopadhyaya, having lived in an east Bengal village, passed through the earlier stages of a successful academic career with unusual rapidity. He studied in Edinburgh, earned his doctorate in 1877, and returned to India to resume his natural vocation. He headed the Nizam College, a premier institution in Hyderabad, and made his mark as a scholar, teacher, and academic administrator. Even with a science degree, he made it his business to relate, as closely as he could, his work to the guidance of his pupil and the furtherance of education. A modern man, his cosmopolitan outlook was the city's gift to many families, mostly from the qasbas of Awadh, who created, thanks to the stimulus provided by the Nizam, a typically eclectic 'Hyderabadi culture'.

In Hyderabad, one saw the Muslim culture in its essence. The Nizam was tolerant, for he believed in liberty, was curious about other people's points of view, and observed Muharram despite being a Sunni. Sarojini Naidu, without being a scholar, did more than any other individual in Hyderabad to bring some of the important but forgotten books within the mental range of the city's elite. From her school days, she cultivated an interest in language and literature. She learnt enough Persian as a child to write a play. The Nizam, to whom the play was submitted by her father, recognised her talent and financed her education in England. Later, she used Persian and Urdu verses in her speeches and writings, and held forth on the quality of three outstanding Urdu poets—Wali Deccani, whose tomb was desecrated by the vandals in Ahmedabad in February 2002, Mir Taqi

27. Halide Edip, *Inside India* (Delhi, introduced and edited by Mushirul Hasan (Delhi, 2000).
28. Sarojini Naidu called the Khyber Pass 'the Road to Destiny'.

Mir, and Ghalib, the two Delhi poets, She cultivated interest in Sufism, recited Jalaluddin Rumi, the great Sufi poet, and observed Muharram to commemorate the martyrdom of Imam Husain in Karbala (Iraq).

> Out of the sombre shadows,
> Over the sunlit grass,
> Slow in a mad possession
> The shadowy pageants pass....
> Hark, from the brooding silence
> Breaks he wild cry of pain
> Wrung from the heart of the ages
> Ali! Hasan! Husain![29]

Freedom and freshness of outlook gave Sarojini Naidu the astonishing insight to see the significance of compositeness in Indian history. In 1906, at the age of 27, she introduced an amendment at the Indian National Conference substituting 'India' for 'Hindu'. It was carried. In sharp contrast to the prevailing orthodoxies, intolerance, and religious dissent, the Golden Threshold was a haven of liberalism and enlightenment. Like Allahabad's Kashmiri Pandits, such as the Nehrus, the Kunzrus, and the Saprus, the Naidus created an enclave in Hyderabad of creativity embracing mixed cultural traditions. Urbane living is what Aghornath and Varada Sundari Devi enjoyed immensely.

In London and then at Girton College, Cambridge, Sarojini Naidu prepared for the work which was to continue, without haste and without rest, until her death. She sought a guru and found one in Edmund Gosse, her 'dear and ever-remembered Godfather'. He spread an influence which profoundly affected for good the study of English literature. The years spent in England were perhaps the quietest and some of the happiest of her early life. She returned to India, married Govindrajulu Naidu, a medical doctor, and gave birth to four children in quick succession.

In London, she had a wide circle of friends, mostly students, journalists and a few public men. Some members of the Naidu family

29. V.S. Naravane, *Sarojini Naidu: Her Life, Work and Poetry* (Delhi, 1980), p. 87.

were also around: Mrinalini Chattopadhyaya (Sarojini's younger sister) and Asaf Ali, a future Delhi lawyer, who became a close friend. He claimed later that he, Syed Mosain, Motilal's protégé in Allahabad, and Sarojini Naidu became 'a trio'. 'Whether is was Harold Monro's Poetry Bookshop, Poets Club dinners, meetings at Oxford and Cambridge, or at the Lyceum where we stayed for a short time, we were almost invariably together.'

From his and other descriptions, it is clear that Sarojini Naidu had become a kind of sovereign with a large court to which students, in addition to literary personages, flocked from London, Oxford and Cambridge. On one occasion, Sarojini Naidu and Asaf Ali debated the comparative merit of Mohamed Ali and Jinnah. Writes Asaf Ali: 'My zealous advocacy on behalf of Mohamed Ali evoked Sarojini's retort, now proved true: "My Mohammad Ali will go further than your Mohamed Ali."[30]

The 'Naughty Gal' of India

On 2 August 1913, Gopal Krishna Gokhale, spoke at Caxton Hall in London. Sarojini Naidu was present. From that day, Gokhale guided her political journey. His vigorous and stimulating influence had a profound impression on her.

The political turmoil following the swadeshi movement continued until the closure of the war when prices soared and unemployment deepened the people's anxieties. The government, instead of embarking on a policy of political and economic liberalisation, resorted to repression. These developments drew into active public life a number of high-minded men and women whose temperaments and orientations would probably have kept them remote from politics in quieter times. In 1915, the Irish-born Annie Besant conceived the idea of Home Rule and enlisted the support of, among others, Mohammad Ali Jinnah, the future architect of Pakistan. Gokhale had married the daughter of Dinshaw Petit, a Parsi. On Home Rule itself, Sarojini Naidu placed the case before the audience in the following words:

30. G.N.S. Raghavan, *M. Asaf Ali's Memoirs: The Emergence of Modern India* (Delhi, 1994), pp. 102-03

> Remember, whatever may be details of our proposals, whatever may be the facts and factors of practical politics that we contemplate, all depends for its worth, its value, its pre-eminent inspiration on the spirit with which these demands and aspirations are conceived and fulfilled. It is no longer an India of Hindus or an India of Muslims, but it an India of the united Indian Nation, with its culture of five thousand years of Vedas, enriched with the Aryan, Unani, Buddhistic, Hellenic, Roman, Scandinavian and European cultures of the world, which have been wisely absorbed by the Vedic culture of India.[31]

Sarojini Naidu responded to the political currents by joining Annie Besant's Home Rule League; as a student, she had met Annie Besant on the ship sailing to the Great Britain. She returned to India in 1899 and travelled to London again in order to plead for the franchise for women before the Joint Select Committee of Parliament which was debating the Montagu-Chelmsford Reforms. Meanwhile, Gandhi, who she met in London—'a little man with a shaven head ... eating a messy meal of squashed tomatoes and olive oil out of a wooden bowl!'—created a political ferment with his Champaran Satyagraha, followed by the Satyagraha against the Rowlatt Bills. Sarojini, as an ardent patriot, signed Gandhi's 'Satyagraha Pledge' against the Rowlatt Act. On 29 October 1921, she endorsed the manifesto declaring that the duty of every Indian soldier and civilian was to sever his connections with the government.[32] In March 1922 she attended the Great Trial in the court of Justice Broomfield. She wrote movingly in the *Bombay Chronicle*:

> A convict and a criminal in the eyes of the law; nevertheless the entire court rose in an act of spontaneous homage when Mahatma Gandhi entered—a frail, serene, indomitable figure in a coarse and scanty loin cloth, accompanied by his devoted disciple and fellow-prisoner, Shankerlal Banker.....'So you are

31. M.R. Jayakar, *The Story of My Life* (Delhi, 1958), vol. 1, p. 202.
32. The other signatories were: Gandhi, C.R. Das, Motilal, Lajpat Rai, Vallabhbahi Patel and C.R.

> seated near me to give me your support in case I break down,' he jested, with that happy laugh of his which seems to hold the undimmed radiance of the world's childhood in its depths, and looking round at all who had come, he said: 'This is like a family gathering and not a law-court.[33]

Progressively, she became more and more involved in the freedom struggle, and, as a woman of special talent, she became the prized trophy of the Congress. She projected the 'modern' face of Indian womanhood, confident, assertive and politically motivated. In an otherwise all-male delegation, she visited Punjab in March 1923 to study the deterioration in the communal situation. She was depressed with the escalation of communal violence and the growing frictions in the Congress over the establishment of the Swaraj Party, but she was not the one to dampen her spirits. 'Let us go on churning the ocean till we do evolve some supreme gift of Harmony', she wrote to Nehru from the Taj Mahal Hotel, her favourite haunt in Bombay.[34] For M.C. Chagla, the lawyer, the hotel was 'a sort of Mecca' to which he returned.[35] There were innumerable days and evenings spent in her room—always the same—talking to her. Here, he'd also meet Ruttie, who was estranged from her husband, Jinnah. He was 'enchanted by her grace, her beauty, and the uninhibited way in which she conducted herself.'[36]

These were precisely the qualities which Sarojini Naidu produced in abundance. Gandhi wanted to propose her name for the presidentship of the Belgaum Congress. But his colleagues thought otherwise and pressed him to take it up himself. G.D. Birla, for instance, told Gandhi that he thought she wasn't a suitable candidate, but the Mahatma stood his ground and argued that she was a very capable leader.[37] Accordingly, in 1925, she was pitchforked into the Congress presidency. Aldous Huxley, the English writer, was present in Kanpur when she spoke. What he saw he described, including Sarojini Naidu consoling the nation in agony.

---

33. Sengupta, Padmini *Sarojini Naidu: A Biography*, (New York, 1966) pp. 169-70.
34. Jawaharlal Nehru (ed.), *A Bunch of Old Letters* (Delhi, 1988, Centenary edition), p. 25.
35. M.C. Chagle, *Roses in December* (Delhi, 1973), p. 89.
36. Ibid., p. 121.
37. Medha M. Kudaisya, *The Life and Times of G.D. Birla* (Delhi, 2003), p. 91.

This is what she said: 'I, who have rocked the cradle—I who have sung soft lullabies—I, the emblem of Mother India, am now to kindle the flame of liberty....In electing me chief among you, through a period fraught with grave issues and fateful decisions, you have reverted to an old tradition and restored to Indian women the classic epoch of our country's history.'[38]

The next year, Sarojini Naidu told the women at the Prayag Mahila Samiti, an organisation concerned with women's education and political participation, that they were the custodians of the destiny of race and must exercise their rights.[39] Sometime during the year, Gandhi vowed 'not to accept any public engagement', and not to leave the Sabarmati Ashram in Ahmedabad. Sarojini Naidu addressed one of her letters to him in July 1926, 'From the Wandering Singer to The Spinner-Stay-At-Home, Greetings'.[40]

Honours and distinctions were already showered upon Sarojini Naidu. In 1928, she visited the United States of America and kept Gandhi informed of the freedom fighters in that country. In 1929, she presided over the East Africa Congress in Mombassa, and delivered lectures all over South East Africa. In January 1932, she attended the Round Table Conference as a representative of Indian womanhood; the Congress Working Committee permitted her to go to London as such. Srinivas Sastri, a loyalist, wondered how she was included in the Indian delegation. She replied: 'I came here because my leader Mahatma Gandhi was not quite sure of the wisdom of the East and insisted on his being supported by the immemorial wisdom of the women of the East!'[41]

Gandhi stayed at Muriel Lester's community settlement at Bow in East London, and was looked after by Sarojini Naidu, Mirabehn, C.F. Andrews and Agatha Harrison, the daughter of a Methodist minister. She took part in the salt satyagraha; under her leadership, Imam Saheb of Sabarmati, Ashram, Pyarelal, Narhari Parekh and Manilal Gandhi, 2,500

38. Sengupta, Padmini *Sarojini Naidu: A Biography*, (New York, 1966) p. 177.
39. Suruchi Thapar-Bjorkert, *Women in the Indian National Movement: Unseen Faces and Unheard Voices 1930-42* (Delhi, 2006), p. 65.
40. B.R. Nanda, *In Gandhi's Footsteps: The Life and Times of Jamnalal Bajaj* (Delhi, 1990), p. 128.
41. Tara Ali Baig, *Sarojini Naidu: Portrait of a Patriot*, (1985) p. 57.

volunteers 'attacked' the Dharasana Salt Works, not far from Dandi, on 21 May. They faced the consequences like anybody – several terms of imprisonment. 'Remember,' she told daughter Leilamani from Yervada on 5 March 1933, 'the darkness holds the light within.'

In July 1936, Nehru mooted the idea of setting up a Civil Liberties Union. Rabindranath Tagore agreed to be its honorary president; he suggested Sarojini Naidu's name for the presidency of the council—'an extraordinarily desirable choice'.[42] That very year, on 4 September, she and G.B. Pant were made members of the Congress Working Committee.

In theory, the national movement paid adequate attention to women's rights, and declared clearly, in the Karachi resolutions (1931) and elsewhere, that there should be no disqualification on the grounds of sex in the exercise of any public function. Yet, in July 1936, women complained against the Congress' indifference towards the questions affecting women.[43] Indeed, male voices dominated the nationalist discourse, although Sarojini Naidu crossed the gender gap, sought new paths of empowerment, and redefined religion and gender relations. Again, in a world dominated by male interpreters of Islam and Hinduism, she asserted her right to interpret religion and to criticise Muslim and non-Muslim scholars alike. She was a liberal voice whose writings spanned many of the major issues facing a resurgent, modern India.

Most people either warmed up to Sarojini Naidu instantly or were spellbound by her talent and vitality. She, too, admired the bold and constructive work of others. She admired, for example, Jinnah's efforts to promote national unity. In early 1913 she travelled to Lucknow, joining Jinnah on the platform as an honoured guest at the Muslim League meeting. Gokhale told her before he died that Jinnah 'has true stuff in him, and that freedom from all sectarian prejudice which will make him the best ambassador of Hindu-Muslim unity.'[44] At the 1915 session of the Congress she recited, in Jinnah's honour, her poem 'Awake'. In December 1916, when the Congress-League Pact was signed, she described him as the ambassador of Hindu-Muslim unity. She believed that his searching

42. On the Indian Civil Liberties Union, S. Gopal (ed.), *Selected Works of Jawaharlal Nehru*, vol. 7, pp. 425-429.
43. Ibid., pp. 313-14.
44. Stanley Wolpert, *Jinnah of Pakistan* (Delhi, 1984)), p. 35.

and quintessentially 'secular' mind led him to cooperate with the Congress at that juncture. This is what she thought of him:

> Never was there a nature whose outer qualities provided so complete an antithesis of its inner work. Tall and stately, but thin to the point of emaciation, languid and luxurious of habit, Mohamed Ali Jinnah's attenuated form is the deceptive sheath of a spirit of exceptional vitality and endurance. Somewhat formal and fastidious, and a little aloof and imperious of manner, the calm hauteur of his accustomed reserve but marks—for those who know him a native and eager humanity, an intuition quick and tender as a woman's, a humour gay and winning as a child's. Pre-eminently rational and practical, discreet and dispassionate in his estimate and acceptance of life, the obvious sanity and serenity of his worldly wisdom effectually disguise a shy and splendid idealism which is the very essence of the man.[45]

In August-September 1928, the Nehru Report was under serious discussion, 'Sarojini,' Motilal, the chief author, told Sarojini Naidu, 'it's your business now to bring Jinnah back [from the All-Parties Conference].'[46] She couldn't. Years later, she spoke of Jinnah as of Lucifer, a fallen angel, one who had once promised to be 'a great leader of Indian freedom, but had instead, cast himself out of the Congress heaven.'[47]

Sarojini Naidu had the art of making friends and acquaintances. She clung to Ansari, Syed Mahmud, the Bihar politician, Shuaib Qureshi,[48] M.C. Chagla, the lawyer-jurist, Shaukat Ali, and other Muslim leaders.

---

45. Kanji Dwarkadas, *India's Fight for Freedom*, pp. 63-64.
46. Shiva Rao, op.cit. Ansari to Jawaharlal, 29 March 1928, AICC papers (G-60); Motilal to Thakurdas, 28, 29 April 1928, Thakurdas Papers (71), NMML.
47. Wolpert, *Jinnah of Pakistan*, p. 289.
48. 'I had met Shuaib Qureshi many times with Mrs. Naidu of whom he was a great favourite. He had also been very close to Gandhiji who at one time had nominated him and Jawaharlalji as Joint Secretaries of the Congress. But he had started drifting away after the All Parties National Convention in Calcutta in 1927 at which the Muslims were prepared to accept joint electorates but which broke down on the issue whether they should have 33 $^{1/3}$% or 30% of the seats in the Central Legislature. Shuaib then entered the service of the Nawab of Bhopal whose Private Secretary he became.' Baig, *In Different Saddles*, pp. 94-5.

Once, Maulana Shaukat Ali and a Hindu leader were arguing violently over some point. A deadlock has been reached, and Sarojini Naidu appealed to the Hindu leader to be generous. 'All right', he said to Maulana, 'who can refuse Mrs. Naidu? I'll go the whole hog and agree to what you ask.' But by now the Maulana's temper was up. 'What do you mean by the whole hog,' he cried, 'Why not the whole bull, the whole beef, the whole cow!'[49]

Sarojini Naidu took pride in her friends. They were all professionals who spoke fluent English, quoted Shakespeare and Wordsworth, and took pride in their network of social connections. It was her nature to be friendly, and like Motilal Nehru, she got over the gulf between generations by ignoring it. In 1937, Tagore pleaded for changing the mindset in order to move to a new era of Hindu-Muslim relationship. He noted: 'In the manner in which Europe emerged from the middle ages and entered the modern era through the pursuit of truth and by expanding the frontiers of knowledge, Hindus and Muslims will have to venture forth from the walls hemming them in.'[50] For Sarojini Naidu, too, national unity and 'united front' remained her overriding concerns. Always, she'd lay stress on the beauty of harmony, concord, and Hindu-Muslim unity.[51]

Gandhi, in spite of his misgivings about the West, engaged in the process of conceptualised pluralism to balance the West with the Eastern social and cultural milieu. Nehru and Abul Kalam Azad made a special effort to recognise 'Western' perspectives and approaches in the concrete world of nation-building. Tagore tried balancing the affirmation of separate identities and a sense of the universal human community, and, using his extraordinary imagination and breadth of vision, he sought to identify areas of East-West cooperation. These divergent approaches produced what might be called a cultural renaissance that became an essential foundation for a strong secular democracy and, even more, a necessary part of a multi-religious society.

49. Ibid, p. 91.
50. Fakhrul Islam & Radha Chakravarty, *The Essential Tagore* (New Delhi, 2011), p. 182.
51. Jawaharlal Nehru, *An Autobiography*, (New York, 1941) p. 594.

Sarojini Naidu incorporated the most eclectic trends in the Gandhi-Tagore-Nehru-Azad approaches. She built bridges of cooperation to create a globalised culture. She went beyond diversity and distinctiveness for making a strong case for tolerance. Tolerance was not just virtuous but, in the long run, a necessity for human survival. She was a nationalist as well as an internationalist with a deep sense of commitment to transcending but not eliminating differences.

Mickey Mouse

'Ah! You must be Mrs Naidu! Who else dare be so irreverent? Come and share my meal!' Gandhi is reported to have said to Sarojini Naidu. They met in London on 8 August 1914. Gandhi had gone there to organise an ambulance corps during World War I. 'And so, laughingly,' recalled Sarojini Naidu on the occasion of Gandhi's 78th birthday, 'we began a friendship that has lasted, grown and developed through all these many years'. Gandhi's simple and austere life inspired the combined feeling of reverence and awe, though the world didn't know, so said Sarojini Naidu jokingly, what it cost to keep the mahatma in poverty. She wore coarse khadi and gave Gandhi over 25 years of devotion. She was the one person who helped him relax and enjoy a joke. She even nicknamed him 'Mickey Mouse'; he enjoyed this and asked all sorts of questions about Mickey Mouse, whom he never had seen on the screen.

In some cases, the smallest details of Gandhi's behaviour served as a model for his followers. Did Sarojini Naidu follow his rules in diet? She cried out: 'Good heavens, all that grass and goat milk? Never, never, never!'[52] She was the only one who could joke with him on his views of *brahmacharya,* chastity. Once when an article appeared in *Young India* suggesting several ways of avoiding the temptation of being with women, the writer advised, among other things, the wearing of dark glasses. As C.R. Rajagopalachari always wore very dark glasses, Sarojini Naidu would make all kinds of naughty remarks about him in which both Gandhj and CR himself would join. CR's views on the subject were as staunch as Gandhi's, but both put up with her teasing.[53]

52. Padmini Sengupta, *Sarojini Naidu: A Biography* (New York, 1966) p. 344.
53. Vijaya Lakshmi Pandit, *The Scope of Happiness* (New Delhi, 1979), pp. 42-43.

The ideology which provided millions of Indians with their purposes in life was, after all, dependent on Gandhi. Sarojini Naidu knew this. Indeed, if a prize had been offered for human devotedness, she might have had to divide the honours with just a handful. She was struck by his single-mindedness, consistency, his good faith, and large-heartedness. Above all, she discovered in him a 'poet in action'—a deliverer from bondage of an ancient, proud people, whom he had taught to stand erect—and a heart as tender and motherly as her own. As a man, he was perfect and beyond criticism. He remained the symbol of India's ideological unity.[54]

From South Africa, 'the cradle of satyagraha', Sarojini Naidu applauded in early 1924: 'I cannot sleep in South Africa and it's all your fault. You haunt the land and its soil is impregnated with the memory of your wonderful struggle, sacrifice and triumph.'[55] 'The Little Man,' she reported to Jawaharlal Nehru from Calcutta in mid-November 1937, 'is sitting unconcernedly eating spinach while the world ebbs and flows about him breaking into waves of Bengali, Gujarati, English and Hindi. ... He is really ill ... not only in his brittle bones and thinning blood but in the core of his soul ... the most lonely and tragic figure of his time.'[56] If many saw him as a saint, others thought of him, to quote her, as 'a fanciful dreamer of inconvenient and impossible dreams.' One of them was Hindu-Muslim unity. Sarojini Naidu was concerned with the 'communal readjustments' and wondered, from her sick bed in The Golden Threshold, if the 'Gandhi Magic' and the 'Nehru Nerves' were ever going to work.[57]

Both in religion and politics, the source of every action is some individual person. Gandhi inspired women and the middle class to straddle the domestic and the public spheres with ease. Thus, the mother of the Ali brothers, the wife of Maulana Hasrat Mohani, Begum Ansari, Attia Fyzee and many other ladies jumped into the fray during the Khilafat movement. Many more responded to Gandhi's non-cooperation movement in 1920-21. Avantikabai Gokhale and Kamaladevi

54. Pyarelal Nayyar, *Mahatma Gandhi: The Last Phase*, vol. 1 (Ahmedebad, 1956), p. 185.
55. "Sarojini Naidu to Gandhi," 29 Feb. 1924, in Paranjape (ed.), *Sarojini Naidu*, p. 172.
56. Sarojini Naidu to Jawaharlal Nehru, 13 November 1937, *A Bunch of Old Letters*, p. 255.
57. Ibid., 29 March 1938, p. 282.

Chattopadhyay were among the first women satyagrahis a decade later. Sarojini Naidu did not lag behind as the head of the Rashtriya Stree Sabha, an independent women's organisation. I reproduce two excerpts from her speeches in 1930 and 1931:

> Till now we have been spectators, but now we have to do something. What your duties are you all know. You have to displace the throne of Britain. Do not think of yourselves as small girls. You are the powerful *Durgas* in disguise. You shall sing the nationalist songs wherever you go. You shall cut the chain of Bondage. And free your country. Forget about the earth. You shall move the skies.
>
> I am an Indian warrior, who is fighting for the freedom of my motherland. All of you are fighting for the protection of your own motherlands. In other words our cause is the same. Consequently, we belong to the same family.[58]

Whenever Gandhi embarked on a fast, she'd worry. Invariably, she'd join him and pray silently for his long life. She was by his side on 20 September 1932, when Gandhi embarked on his fast against the provision of separate electorates in the communal award. Her daughter Padmaja, the 'Lotus Maiden' thought he was witnessing 'a catharsis' cleansing Hinduism of 'the accumulated corruption of centuries.'[59] On 10 February 1943, Gandhi commenced his fast, which he ended on 2 March 1943. A relieved Sarojini Naidu referred to the problem and paradox of 'the marvellous little Mickey Mouse who has nibbled his way back to life from the lightly spread and knotted nets of death.' She told her daughter 'of his 'horrid scrubby little chin growth which made him look like a gnome and he had himself shaved and trimmed to "look nice" because he thought I was being rude about his appearance.'[60]

During the Quit India movement, women from the middle class answered Gandhi's call with the same degree of patriotic fervour.

58. Thapar-Bjorkert, *Women in the Indian National Movement*, pp. 84-5.
59. Rajmohan Gandhi, *Mohandas: A True Story of a Man, His People and an Empire* (Delhi, 2006), p. 373.
60. "To Leilamani Naidu", 3 March 1943, in Paranjape (ed), *Sarojini Naidu*, p. 309

There was thunder in the air. Sarojini Naidu sniffed that thunder and anticipated mass arrest to take place. She prepared herself in her Bombay house for the eventual arrest. The bell rang at 4 a.m. The police came in. Her hunch proved right. She and others were led into prison on 8 August 1942. For Beverley Nichols, an otherwise unsympathetic observer of Indian political trends, it was 'more interesting to consider her merely as a cultured, charming woman, swept into gaol as the result of her convictions.'[61]

'Being guarded like a jewel in a casket'

Sarojini Naidu found prison life to be monotonous. The rooms were pleasant, the food was good, and the British were most polite but they were utterly isolated. For three weeks they had not a scrap of news. All the papers were banned, and there was no radio; even their families had no idea where they had been taken.

Now and then, of course, there were brighter moments; one of them occurred when C. Rajagopalachari, himself an ex-President of Congress, came to visit Gandhi. The last time C.R. had seen him, Gandhi had been reading *The Hound of Heaven,* and Sarojini Naidu had been sitting by him trying to explain what it all meant. 'Well,' said C.R. 'have you finished that dog poem yet?'

Perhaps the most dramatic thing Sarojini Naidu told Nichols was about Gandhi's famous fast of February 1943. A number of unsavoury things have been said about that fast; it was suggested that the state of the Mahatma's health chart varied according to the political situation, that when the Viceroy looked like yielding, Gandhi grew rapidly worse, and when the Viceroy appeared adamant, Gandhi took a marked turn for the better. According to Nichols, 'our contempt for this form of political masochism does not justify us in assuming that it was a fake.'

Sarojini Naidu, at least, had a very different story to tell. She said that towards the end of the seventh day, Gandhi, to all appearances died. He had been sinking rapidly since the morning; they were gathered round his bedside, fearing the worst. As the dusk deepened the worst seemed to happen; his breathing ceased, his pulse faltered and stopped.

61. Beverley Nichols, *Verdict on India*, p. 152.

'It was as though a light had gone out of the world,' she said. How he came back, by what miracle the frail, wizened body reasserted itself, she couldn't explain; she was too moved by the memory of it. All she could suggest was that it was a supreme effort of will.

Conclusion

Sarojini Naidu was deflected from the highway of poetry by her engagement in politics. Her first slim volume of poetry appeared in 1905. I cannot judge her as a poet for I read next to no English poetry, but I do know that her fame had spread by gradual and incessant effort. Her three books, *The Golden Threshold* (1905), *The Bird of Time* (1912) and later, *The Broken Wing* (1917), were well received in India and England. *The Golden Threshold,* in particular, received complimentary reviews in *The London Times* and *The Manchester Guardian. The Sceptred Flute* appeared in 1937. Bubbling with wit, humour and charm, she was potentially a poet of major rank,

The range of her essays and reviews is limited, but she could write judicially because, unlike certain creative writers who scatter their energy to little purpose, Sarojini Naidu saw the interplay of the intellectual and the political. Her prose is not far from its best in the passages of her presidential address delivered at the Kanpur session of the Indian National Congress in 1925. She set out to describe a society which she saw and which suffered under colonial rule. This body of material has a certain unity which says much for her singleness of aim.

'True as the peach to its ripening taste/Is destiny to her hour'. Like the poet's deep and unwavering faith in the future, Sarojini Naidu foresaw and foretold the day of freedom. She saw the flag of freedom on the rampart of the Red Fort, but she also saw men, women, and children being uprooted by the outbreak of ferocious violence. She saw the festivities being overtaken by a massive tragedy—the assassination of the 'Father of the Nation.' For her, who did more than most to bring out the light and colour in his life, the most poignant and memorable of all was the last picture of his walking to his prayers at the sunset hour, translated in a tragic instant of martyrdom from mortality to immortality.[62] When finally,

62. Padmini Sengupta, *Sarojini Naidu: A Biography*, (New York, 1966) op.cit., p. 345.

Gandhi succumbed to bullet wounds on 30 January, 1948, she sang his glory and enumerated the marvels which attested his mission.

> The most epic event of modern times ended quickly. The pent-up emotion of the people burst in a storm of sorrow, as a long, slow procession moved towards Gandhi in a mournful pilgrimage of farewell, clinging to the hands that had toiled so incessantly, bowing over the feet that had journeyed so continuously in the service of his country. In the midst of all this poignant scene of many-voiced and myriad-hearted grief, he stood, untroubled, in all his transcendent simplicity, the embodied symbol of the Indian Nation-its living sacrifice and sacrament in one.
>
> They might take the Mahatma to the utmost ends of the earth, but his destination remains unchanged in the hearts of his people who are both the heirs and stewards of his matchless dreams and his matchless deeds.

She made a moving broadcast to a shocked nation on 1 February 1948, ending with the stirring words, 'My father, do not rest. Keep us to our pledge, give us the strength to fulfil our promise, your heirs, your descendants, your stewards, the guardians of your dreams, the fulfillers of India's destiny. You whose life was so powerful, make it as powerful in your death. For from mortality you have passed to immortality by supreme martyrdom in the cause most dear to you: Hindu-Muslim friendship.'

Sarojini Naidu saw herself as an individual whose experiences, opinions, and inner feelings had a right to be heard, and are certainly worth hearing. She wrote poetry; the poetry of love and pleasure, laughter and tears. She talked things over with Gandhi, who called her *Bharat Kokila*—India's Nightingale—that she would never have thought of discussing with any other man. There was something very beautiful in their relationship; so closely and constantly were they linked together. Endowed as he was with the liveliest sensibility to feminine influence, his life of self-discipline and self-development, and, as he aptly called it, self-abandon, he welded together in his own person the masculine and feminine qualities into a single whole, free from tension.[63] He deliberately surrounded himself with women to prove that his mastery over 'lust' was not achieved by avoiding them.[64]

The Nightingale's voice was stilled on 2 March 1949. As the Governor of Uttar Pradesh, Sarojini Naidu used to jest, 'I am a Governess'. As in life, she would have faced death with a light heart and with a song on the lips and smile on the face.

The printed word ends here, but Sarojini Naidu's living story continues. I hope the younger generations would recognise that, 'just as the Father of the Nation had infused moral grandeur and greatness into the struggle, Mrs Sarojini Naidu gave it artistry and poetry.' Hopefully, they will honour her patriotism, her zest for life, her energy and drive. In the words of Halide Edip:

> ... This gift of words and their magic use has been at the service of India's independence movement for over twenty years, electrifying audiences from one end of the country to the other, almost hypnotising them into believing in a free India. As to the form that independence will take, and how Indian society must prepare for it, that is not necessarily the subject of her speeches. She is the earliest of the sowers of the seed and without her modern India is inconceivable. And I can't think of her without remembering the lines from Shakespeare:
> *Age cannot wither her, nor custom stale*
> *Her infinite variety.*[65]

---

63 Horace Alexander, *Consider India: An Essay in Values* (Calcutta, 1961) p. 58.

64. Louis Fischer, *The Life of Mahatma Gandhi*, (New York, 1950) p. 440.

65. Halide Edip, *Inside India*. Introduced and edited by Mushirul Hasan (New Delhi, 2000) p. 28.

Portrait of a young Sarojini Naidu (née Chattopadhyaya) in the early 1900s. (Nehru Memorial Museum & Library, New Delhi)

Sarojini Naidu at the Lucknow Congress with Ambika Charan Mazumdar and others in 1916. (Nehru Memorial Museum & Library, New Delhi)

M.K. Gandhi and Sarojini Naidu on the way to Buckingham Palace to meet King George V for the Second Round Table Conference September-December 1931. (Nehru Memorial Museum & Library, New Delhi)

Jawaharlal Nehru, Subhash Chandra Bose and Sarojini Naidu sharing a meal in 1938. This was the same year Bose became President of Congress. (Nehru Memorial Museum & Library, New Delhi)

Sarojini Naidu giving a talk at a function in Chicago, 1938. (Nehru Memorial Museum & Library, New Delhi)

Jawaharlal Nehru with Sarojini Naidu, 1938. (Nehru Memorial Museum & Library, New Delhi)

Sarojini Naidu with Jawaharlal Nehru, Edwina Mountbatten and her daughter Pamela and Padmaja Naidu in 1947. (Nehru Memorial Museum & Library, New Delhi)

Sarojini Naidu as Governor of Uttar Pradesh, 1949. (Nehru Memorial Museum & Library, New Delhi)

PART ONE

Sarojini Naidu—Some Facets of Her Personality*

Sarojini Naidu as a Freedom Fighter

by **P.K. Ghosh**

Born in Hyderabad, Sarojini Naidu was the first among the subjects of Princely India who rose to the stature of a national leader. She personified in her a rare harmony of a poet and a patriot. Freedom was her life's lyric.

Sarojini had gifted parents. Her father, Dr. Aghorenath Chattopadhyaya was a Brahmo who grew up in the climate of 19th century renaiscent Bengal. He combined in himself love of learning and high-mindedness. Sarojini, besides absorbing intellectual influences at home, inherited her father's courage and love of truth. From her mother, Varada Sundari Devi, she inherited the poetic gift.

She had already earned the reputation of a poetess by twenty-one years' of age. She did not choose the seclusion of an ivory tower. She was to be drawn into the grim world of politics. In 1904 she attended the Congress session at Bombay as an observer. But the first event that hurt her sense of justice was the partition of Bengal in 1905. Curzon's resolve to partition the Bengal Presidency and thereby divide the Bengali speaking population was considered as an affront and a challenge to be met. She left for Bengal and plunged herself headlong into the anti-partition agitation. The movement gained momentum and generated anti-British feeling as much among the elites as among the masses. It was a formative period for many who were to play significant roles in the nationalist struggle later on. Sarojini, too was drawn in and she partook of the popular moods. At the Calcutta Session in 1906 the identities of so-called Moderates and Extremists within the Congress were clearly marked off. Sarojini spoke at the Congress platform but

* The essays in this section originally appeared in a book titled *Sarojini Naidu: Some Facets of Her Personality,* published by the National Archives of India in 1979.

without identifying herself with either Camp. However, her role as a constitutionalist of the Moderate brand was soon established. In the Congress crisis of 1907 she was drawn towards Gopal Krishna Gokhale and followed the political philosophy he espoused. In 1914, during her visit to London, as Gokhale's emissary she was attracted by Gandhiji and for the rest of her life she remained loyal to him. Thus her role as a political worker was clearly defined—self government and inter-communal harmony. To this she added the emancipation of women her special sphere of action.

In defining her public role, one is conscious that one is casting this mercurial personality in a straight jacket. In fact all causes which stemmed from the desire to ameliorate the condition of Indians anywhere in the world elicited her deepest response. She collaborated with C.F. Andrews in his crusade to remove the grievances of the distressed indentured Indian labour in South Africa.

But her main platform was the congress from where she could express her feelings or project her ideas on specific issues. At the Lucknow session (December 1916) Sarojini moved a resolution against the disgraceful Arms Act. The Montagu-Chelmsford Reforms were considered a half measure which did not satisfy nationalist India. But the introduction of Rowlatt Bills in the Council generated unprecedented agitation in the country. The Punjab tragedy wounded the nationalist heart at its deepest. India was restless and hypersensitive. Mrs. Naidu was touched to the quick by the tragedy and she felt the national disgrace much more keenly than she did at the partition of Bengal. Anglo-Indian bureaucracy at heat applauded General Dyer for his action at the Jallianwala Bagh. Finding that justice was not to be had in India, Sarojini Naidu joined a select deputation to Britain in July 1919 to protest against the severities of martial law administration and in particular to seek justice for the outraged women of the Punjab. On 3rd June 1920 she made a speech at the Kingsway Hall in London on the 'agony and shame of the Punjab'. The upshot of the debate in the House of Commons left her still more disenchanted with the Raj. She wrote to the Secretary of State, Edwin Montagu and impressed upon him that the Congress sub-committee's report on the Punjab atrocities was factually correct. The reply she received characterized the allegations as 'wholly untrue'. The next day the same official replying on behalf of Montagu admitted some of the allegations and added that the offenders were subordinate police officials. Unimpressed by the lifeless debate in the Commons, Sarojini wrote to Gandhiji that she had lost all faith in the British sense of justice. In July 1921 she returned to India totally disillusioned.

Gandhiji had, in the meanwhile, launched the Non-Cooperation Movement. Although the Congress at its Calcutta and Nagpur Sessions in September and December 1920 had endorsed the movement, it was only at the end of 1921 that it was formally launched beginning with the demonstration in Bombay against the visiting Prince of Wales. Although Sarojini did not court arrest, she was actively involved in it to make the British boycott a success. As a believer in non-violence, she was even engaged in quelling the riots in Bombay. Being a signatory to the Non-Cooperation Manifesto, she was committed to Gandhiji's programme.

In January 1924 Mrs. Naidu visited Africa and presided over the East African Indians Congress at Mombassa. She was invited again in November 1929 to preside over the same Congress. Both the sessions were inspired by the apartheid laws based on racial discrimination. She visited United States as an envoy of nationalist India to enlist support for the cause of freedom.

She had gained stature and was a front rank leader now. In 1925 she was elected to preside over the Congress session at Kanpur. Nothing spectacular happened during this period until towards the close of the decade. In December 1929 the Congress declared complete independence as its goal. Gandhiji also decided to launch the Civil Disobedience Movement. As a test case he decided to break the salt laws at Dandi.

The Salt Satyagraha and the march to Dandi began to grow in people's imagination. Satyagrahis flocked to Gandhiji's march and on April 6 he broke the salt laws by making salt from sea water. He was arrested. The leadership of the movement fell on Abbas Tyabji and after his arrest on Mrs. Naidu.

Mrs. Naidu went to Dharasana. As was planned satyagrahis were to take part in a raid. This was followed by series of raids on the Wadala salt depot. The most spectacular of the raid took place on 1st June wherein

15,000 volunteers participated in the action. The American newsman Webb Miller recorded in detail this great event. Dr. R.C. Majumdar observes:

"His (Miller's) description has an epic grandeur about it, and will go down in history as the finest memorial of the martyrs of civil disobedience launched by Gandhi in 1930".

The assemblage of the volunteers near Dharasana made the Government somewhat anxious. The area was cut off from the rest of the world and steps were taken to prevent news going out of the place. Miller himself was forced out of the train at Bulsar. With difficulty he reached Dungeri, the railway station near Dharasana and met Sarojini and her non-violent army. They continued the march till they were stopped by the police. The volunteers were severely beaten. They were cordoned off by the police. The young volunteers remained undeterred by hunger and thirst. Among them sat under the hot summer sun brave and smiling Sarojini Naidu. Miller reports, "Mme. Naidu called for prayer before the march started and the entire assemblage knelt. She exhorted them, 'Gandhi's body is in jail but his soul is with you. India's prestige is in your hands. You must not use violence under any circumstances. You will be beaten but you must not resist, you must not raise a hand to ward off blows. Wild, shrill cheers terminated her speech. Slowly in silence the throng commenced the halfmile march"

The club of the policeman fell on the volunteers. Despite their merciless beating, the marchers remained non-violent. Sarojini was arrested and sent to prison. Dharasana will always remain as *the* event in the story of salt satyagrah. It was first time Sarojini had the taste of police action and she was prepared to face it with courage.

Her faith in Gandhiji's leadership was absolute. She remained close to him as an unquestioning disciple. She went with him to Britain to attend the Round Table Conference. She was with him when Gandhiji went on fast in the Yervada jail. She was imprisoned with him in the Agha Khan Palace in Pune. In 1943 she was released. In fact she was the first among the Congress Working Committee members to come out of jail.

Freedom from foreign rule was welcome but the division of India and the consequences that flowed from it left Mrs. Naidu a sad person.

Despite this she wore a cheerful expression. As governor of United provinces she immersed herself in the task of consolidation of that freedom and in the developmental programmes of her charge. The oratorical gifts which she had so amply and successfully employed in her addresses during the freedom struggle were no less helpful in the successful performance of her new role. Mrs. Naidu was courageous woman. She combined in herself the roles of a housewife, a poet, a politician and a social reformer. It was the saga of a complete life.

Sarojini Naidu's Views on Social Issues of Her Time

by **Bina Roy**

> "When the terror and tumult of hate shall cease
> And life be refashioned on avails of peace,
> And your love shall offer memorial thanks
> To the comrades who fought in your dauntless ranks,
> And your honour the deeds of the deathless ones,
> Remember the blood of my martyred son.."
>
> *The Gift of India*
> by Sarojini Naidu

I

This verse reflects the personality that Sarojini Naidu was—a poet turned politician. However, Nissim Ezekiel, reviewing her collection of poems *The Feather of the Dawn* says, "Sarojini knew nothing of the literary revolutions taking place in English poetry in the twenties and earlier".[1] Exactly a year ago, on the date and about the same time, Mrs. Lakshmi Menon delivered a talk at the Nehru Memorial Museum and Library, at the beginning of the year long celebrations of the centenary of her birth. She mentioned Mrs. Naidu's response to some questions raised by Aldous Huxley," "... people insist on calling me a politician when I never pretended to be one. It is really an irony of fate and a joke".[2]

In analyzing this issue, Mrs. Menon brought out that the true approach needed to understand Mrs. Naidu is to realise that she was a true humanist who loved people with all their joys and sorrows. She draws the conclusion that owing to this humane attitude towards social

1. *Sunday Standard,* Feb. 11, 1962.
2. Manuscript at Nehru Memorial Library.

problems in India, she became the bard leading and inspiring the masses in their freedom movement under Mahatma Gandhi.

Gandhiji considered that in our freedom movement five things needed attention: (i) non-violence, (ii) khadi (iii) Hindu-Muslim unity (iv) Harijans and (v) women. In the pre-Independence period, it was not possible to keep these five strands strictly separate. It was a theory expected to be realised in life in free India. Needless to say that all these five points of work for national regeneration are meant basically to improve the social life of the Indian people as a whole.

During the years immediately following independence in 1947 one often heard and read about the stages in which true and complete freedom will be achieved. The first stage had just been completed with the achievement of political freedom, i.e. the decision making power now belonged to the Indian people to shape and direct the course of their destiny. The second stage was that of economic freedom which was expected to be achieved on the basis of free India's own political decisions. Finally, the third stage of social liberation was expected to be the normal consequence of political and economic freedom.

Sarojini Naidu was caught up in this movement led by Mahatma Gandhi to usher in a new India of social equality. She not only dreamed of it and worked for it in the Gandhian movement, but she lived up to everything she proposed. She talked and inspired millions to break down social barriers. She was only too conscious of the existing barriers, but being involved in the struggle to win the first stage of freedom, she had no time to concentrate on any single area of activity. However, she expressed a sincere concern for all the existing social problems of her time and lost no opportunity to point these out to those who were actively involved in removing social evils. She expressed with her eloquent power what she expected Indian society to be.

Of the five points mentioned by Gandhiji, non-violence, khadi and Hindu-Muslim unity were activities which got intermingled with and overcharged with the political issues of the first phase of the freedom movement. The question of harijans and women remained in the background as purely social issues. One other aspect of social issue, received her special attention, viz., her approach to the youth of India.

In her writings and speeches referring to India's regeneration, two things stand out. The first one is that these efforts, large or small each trying to remedy one type of social problem, were like small feeders swelling the fast flowing river of the national movement; the other was that her expressions were poetic in language and inspiration. It was impossible to separate Mrs. Naidu's views on social issues from the national movement and/or her poetry. I reproduce only one of these;

At Dawn[3]
Children, my children, the daylight is breaking,
The cymbals of morn sound the hour of your waking,
The long night is o'er, and our labour is ended,
Fair blow the fields that we tilled and we tended, Swiftly the
harvest grows mellow for reaping,
The harvest we sowed for the time of your sleeping.
Weak were our hands but service was tender,
In darkness we dreamed the dawn of your splendour,
In silence we strove for the joy of the morrow,
And watered your seeds from the wells of our sorrow,
We toiled to enrich the glad hour of your waking,
Our vigil is done, lo ! The daylight is breaking.
Children, my children, who wake to inherit
The ultimate hope of our travailing spirit,
Say, when your young hearts shall take to their keeping,
The manifold dreams have sown for your reaping,
Is it praise, is it pain you will grant us for guerdon?
Anoint with your love or arraign with your pardon?

II

Of the social issues which the leaders of the national movement gave priority to, the one of women received Mrs. Naidu's maximum attention. She symbolised those women who, inspite of a happy life plunged themselves whole heartedly in the new opportunities of work in the larger interests of the nation. In fact wherever she went she was

3. Naidu's *The Sceptred Flute: Songs of India* Allahabad, Kitabistan, 1946, p.129.

recognised as brilliant, charming, challenging, kind and understanding in her approach to all human questions. This recognition came to her not only in India but also in other lands which she visited.

With her insight she understood the joys and sorrows, expectations and hopes of women of all categories including women vendors in cities and rural poor group. In her poems, she reflects the whole range of moods and emotions with superb subtlety of expression. Dr. P.V. Rajyalakshmi points out that this range of moods even comprehends mystic communications, and that her reflections of folk theme show "genuine understanding and appreciation of India's folk culture. She projects totality of others'... customs, beliefs, legends, mimicry, games, festivals...,"[4] One has only to read her little poems on subjects such as "Festival of the Sea", "Gypsy Girl", "Banjara Women", "Zobida" and "Gulnar".

Her speeches have not been recorded carefully for posterity. But some important statements which have been recorded can be said today—30 years after we started using our power for decision making on economic and social issues.

In her speech at a meeting of the Hindu social Reform Association held in Secunderabad in 1906, she said, "Every place has a social reform association. But what have they done? The word 'Today' is not in our dictionary. 'Tomorrow' is the watchword. There is anxiety shown everywhere for the introduction of social reform into families of other but not in one's own family..."[5]

At the 22nd session of the Indian National Social Conference, held in 1908, she inspired a resolution for providing educational facilities for widows, establishment of women's homes and removing obstacles to their remarriage.

On women's education her statements in 1906 and 1908 could be repeated today by those fighting for improving the status of woman in the current International Decade for Women. At the Indian Social Conference held in Calcutta in 1906 she said, "...at this great moment of stress and striving, when Indian races are seeking the ultimate unity of a common national ideal, it is well for us to remember that the success

---

4. Rajyalakshmi, P. V., *The Lyrice Spring*, New Delhi, Abhinav Publications, 1977, p. 183.
5. *Speeches and Writings of Sarojini Naidu*, Madras, p. 22

of the whole movement lies centered in what is known as the *women question*...[6] But it seems to me that there is not even an unanimous acceptance of the fact that education of women is an essential factor in the process of nation building".[7]

Later, in the same conference she referred to a controversy on women's education published in *Indian Ladies Magazine* which reflected that all women expressed themselves for education but there was division in men's camp. While some agreed, "others took fright at the very idea, 'What?, they carried,' education for our women? What then will become of the comfortable domestic 'ideals as exemplified by the luscious *halwa* and savoury *omlette*. Others again were neither for Jove nor Jehova, but for compromise bringing forward a whole syllabus of compromises, "Teach this", they said, "and not that". But my friends, in the matter of education you cannot say thus far and no further. Neither can you say to the winds of heaven, 'Blow not where ye list', nor forbid the waves to cross their boundaries, nor the human soul to soar beyond the bounds of arbitrary limitations".[8]

In 1908, Pandit Madan Mohan Malaviya was giving a talk at the Pachaiappa's College Historical Association. After his speech Mrs. Naidu responded that women in other advanced countries constituted a most potent factor in the political evolution of a country. In India, while men were educated and kept abreast, women were lagging behind.[9]

Under her inspiration, the Women's Indian Association at its conference in 1936, published *Women's Manifesto* to the candidates standing for election to the Provincial and central legislatures and all other public bodies. This could be reproduced and used today by women's organisations in emphasizing the social issues needing legislative and executive action[10].

To the women in their own gathering she would say the same but equally forcefully each time—as she did at the Indian Ladies Club at

6. *Underline* mine.
7. *Speeches* p. 18
8. Underline mine, pp. 18-19.
9. *Speeches*, p.26.
10. Women's Indian Association, *Eighteenth and Nineteenth Report*, 1934-1936, Madras, "Everest", Lahore, 1936, pp. 32-33.

Pittapwam in 1915, "... I say that it is time for us all women of India, to awake, whatever our race, or caste or creed, or rank in life, to awaken and grasp the urgency of the situation in the immediate need of adequate and equal cooperation and comradeship in guiding, moulding, sustaining and achieving those lofty and patriotic ideals that thrill the heart of every generation and whose fulfillment line the noblest destiny of man".[11]

It was under the leadership of Sarojini Naidu and others that the All India women's conference (AIWC) was founded. One of the successful achievement of this organisation was to press for non-communal representation when the British Parliament was preparing for special representation in the constitution of India for minorities. True this move did not succeed against the force in England which ultimately decided the issue at that time. However, it is on record that women of all religions, castes and creeds, through the AIWC made a strong plea for non-communal representation.

Another interesting story which I am not able to authenticate yet with appropriate documentation has reference to the Hindu Code Bill. Before she passed away, she was addressing a meeting at the University Institute Hall in Calcutta organised by some local women's organizations to express their support for the Bill. The orthodox reactionary group crowded the hall in great numbers. Mrs. Naidu was quick enough to sense the situation. In her speech she demolished all orthodox arguments so thoroughly that before her speech ended people were prepared to leave the hall in groups. It is needless to say how the meeting ended after this group chose not to stay.

III

The young generation of men and women were naturally attracted to her for she could talk to each one in his or her own idiom. At the same time, she was concerned that the young men and women of her time would one day inherit the struggle for national freedom and progress and carry it forward. The point that she wanted them to understand is found in her address on "Time Brotherhood" at Pachaiappa's College in 1903.

11. *Speeches*, p. 73.

"... Having travelled... conceived... hoped... having contacts with all communities, religions... civilisations... my vision is clear. I have no prejudice of race, creed, caste or colour... Be an Indian and not a madrasee..."[12]

Her vision was that the young men and women of her country should grow up to be true Indians and rise above narrow local, linguistic, racial and religious identities. She was also aware of the fact that the quality of the nation did not depend on the excellence of a few outstanding persons or a small group of elites. Work had to be done to uplift the masses so that the average quality of the people continue to rise higher. She expressed this in an address entitled "The Hope of Tomorrow" given at the Madras Students Convention.

She was disturbed when she found the youth callous about the state of the country and society and their own responsibility to improve the existing conditions. I witnessed one of these at the main hall of Lucknow University. Mrs. Naidu was expected to arrive any moment. The hall was over-crowded and catcalls started from the gallery above. She was hardly noticed in the crowd. She was up on the platform. By then the noise on the floor of the hall had stopped but not from the gallery. After she was introduced, the first thing she did was to mimic the catcalls, perfect to the last details of sound. The first response was laughter, but Mrs. Naidu looked serious and continued to mimic the catcalls until the students realised that she would speak only when there was complete silence. As she began to speak she literally administered a strongly worded rebuke to students about their lack of responsibility. She reminded them of the work that the Chinese students and students elsewhere were doing for their nation, while Indian students were whiling away their time in futile activities. This was not the first time she noticed shortcoming in the youth. She wrote in the poem entitled "Life":

"Children, ye have not lived, ye but exist
Till some resistless hour shall rise and move
Your hearts to wake and hunger after love
And thirst with passionate longing for the things

12. *ibid*, pp. 9-11.

That burn your brows with blood-red sufferings.
Till ye have battled with great grief and fears,
And borne the conflict of dream shattering years,
Wounded with fierce desire and worn with strife
Children, you have not lived, for this is life".[13]

IV

On poverty and related national economic reconstruction her views are no less relevant in the present context. Mrs. Lakshmi Menon, quotes Mrs. Naidu as having said that a few places, universities and modern appliances are not adequate for the advancement of a nation, "Is this the criterion of progress?" She asked and continued, "no, believe me, your progress, your liberty, your achievement, will only be worth having when there is food in every village".

In her presidential address in 1925 as Congress President she covered the need for village reconstruction and education along with the politically charged issues of non-violent, non-cooperation and Hindu-Muslim unity. She emphasised that national reconstruction needed personal and collective sacrifice, and invisible faith and commitment to the cause of unity of the nation for the struggle ahead—

"With palms uplifted in ardent supplication, I pray that to us in our coming hour of travail may be granted in sufficient measure an invisible faith and inflexible courage, and that He in whose name we begin our labour today will in the hour of our triumph keep us humble and in the beautiful words of our ancient invocation:

"Lead us out of the unreal into the Real
Out of darkness into the light
Out of Death into Immortality".

My own personal memory is still quite vivid about her presence and impact on every one at the 49th session of the Indian National Congress held at Lucknow in 1936. She was personally interested in the welfare of each and every volunteer in the Congress camp she met.

In terms of decisions on national policy for the country's development, the focus was on rural development and improvement

13. Naidu's. *The Sceptred Flute:* p. 35.

of the life style of agricultural labourers and cultivators. The Congress policy adopted in 1936 emphasised the freedom of organisation of agricultural labourers, their emancipation from feudal levies, substantial reduction in rent and revenue, fast and fair relief from agricultural indebtedness and safeguarding their interests vis-à-vis the state, allotment in state expenditure for economic, social and cultural amenities, freedom from oppression and harassment from government officials, protection against restrictions on utilisation of natural facilities for domestic and agricultural needs and, finally, fostering incentive for relieving rural unemployment.

It was truly a revolutionary concept evolved under the leadership of Pandit Jawaharlal Nehru as the then Congress President. At the end of business Pandit Nehru mentioned that, "It is customary on such occasion when all business is over for someone to indulge in a funeral oration. So Mrs. Naidu has come here uninvited to deliver that oration..."

Mrs. Naidu, reflecting on the far reaching decisions of that Congress said.

"In this city of old traditions... we have witnessed the birth of a new vision, the coming of a new dream. I am here on your behalf, to bear testimony to the marvelous miracles that have happened for us and for India. Out of the past has come the future not by resolution but by proper, decent evolution... For the first time has that note been sounded, has that vision been revealed, has that prophecy been made that Congress should realise that India shall be an integral part of the great world scheme of freedom and liberation. And so, if Jawaharlal thinks that it is a funeral oration it is a funeral oration to the dead yesterday but a welcome oration to tomorrow, to the dawn of which the President is the herald... to be able to hold together in friendliness elements which might have been hostile to one another and irreconcilable with one another. Therefore, I end with adieu to yesterday and welcome tomorrow in which we join together in our pilgrimage towards the dawn of liberty". It was past midnight and the session ended with "Vande Mataram" rending the silence of the night.

V

Inspite of her family responsibilities and frail health, she never failed to face the most difficult situations with humility, simplicity and yet conviction and courage. Above all, she was endowed with the healing gift of a sense of humour and pen which resolved tensions within a group. Her ability to laugh at herself and others was so refined and without any malice that she carried individuals and groups with her as no other could.

Some have raised the question, was she pleased with the freedom as it came dividing India and shattering the dream of united free India as dreamed by our freedom fighters. Those who know her intimately feel that she was sad but few sensed it. Yet outwardly she was the same person, full of humour, with time to meet each one at a very personal level. That she knew that life has its set backs and one must be ready for them is reflected also in her writing—e.g. "Conquest"[14] written in 1927 and "The Soul's Prayer"[15] first published in India in 1943 but published elsewhere much earlier.

14. Naidu, S. *The Feather of the Dawn:* New York; Asia Publishing House, 1961, pp. 32-33.
15. Naidu, S. *The Sceptred Flute:* pp. 123-124.

Sarojini Naidu: Her Way with Words

by **V.V. John**

A hundred and one years ago today, was born Sarojini Chattopadhyaya, who became one of the most delightfully articulate spokesmen of India's freedom struggle. Her probation for this role included, strangely, a period during which she wrote romantic lyrics in English and published three volumes of them. For a while, seemingly, she felt that her destiny was to be a singer of songs.

> To priests and to prophets
> The joy of their creeds,
> To Kinds and to cohorts
> The glory of deeds;
> And peace to the vanquished
> And hope to the strong;
> For me, O my Master,
> The rapture of song.

Though the poems disclosed much technical competence, many of them suffered from a certain wordiness that vastly diminishes their appeal to the modern reader of poetry. The romantic raptures makes us feel somewhat uncomfortable. For instance, the much-quoted 'Palanquin-Bearers':

> Lightly, O lightly, we bear her along,
> She sways like a flower in the wind of our song;
> She skims like a bird on the foam of a stream,
> Gaily, O gaily we glide and we sing,
> We bear her along like a pearl on a string.

If Sarojini had returned to the theme in the robustness of outlook that was so characteristic of her in her later years, I guess she would have pictured the palanquin-bearers as suitably unionized and reckoning their burden as not so 'lightly' O lightly; And let us not forget that a major English poet, W.B. Yeats, was, about the same time, rhapsodizing over the Lake Isle of Innisfree ('I will arise and go now, and go to Innisfree') and took years to acknowledge that the object of his raptures was popularly known as Rat Island, and to severely exclude the poem from his own anthology of modern English verse.

Sarojini, the lyricist, knew when to quit. But the disdain in which some are inclined to hold her poetic output is overdone, and discloses an unawareness of some beautiful poems, such as 'The Gift of India' where Sarojini celebrated the heroism of the Indian soldiers that had fallen in battle in the First. World War. Auden's definition of poetry as 'memorable speech' would apply eminently to this beautiful poem, particularly its closing stanza:

> When the terror and tumult of hate shall cease
> And life be refashioned on anvils of peace,
> And your love shall offer memorial thanks
> To the comrades who fought in your dauntless ranks,
> And you honour the deeds of the deathless ones,
> Remember the blood of my martyred sons!

I have been unable to ascertain who first referred to Sarojini Naidu as the nightingale of India. The frailty of her figure and the simple music of her verse must have suggested the appellation. And it stuck, and came up in the most inappropriate contexts. Her robust forthrightness of speech and her indomitable spirit that triumphed over sorrow and sickness, do not exactly conjure up the image of the nightingale, and the cliché did less than justice to her vibrant personality. There was much less of the languishing Lady of Shallot than of the Plain-spoken wife of Bath in her mental make-up. Thinking of her, my irreverent mind has found in her a kinship with the ribald figure of his mother that the poet George Barker celebrates in his poem, 'To My Mother':

Most near, most dear, most loved and most far,
Under the window where I often found her
Sitting as huge as Asia, seismic with laughter,
Gin and chicken helpless in her Irish hand,
Irresitible as Rabelais, but most tender for
The lame dogs and hurt birds that surround her,—
She is a procession no one can follow after
But be like a little dog following a brass band.
She will not glance up at the bomber, or condescend
To drop her gin and scuttle to a cellar,
But lean on the mahogany table like a mountain
Whom only faith can move, and so I send
O all my faith, and all my love to tell her
That she will move from mourning into morning.

May I stress again that his image comes to my mind, not so much because of any physical dimensions, but because of the cheerful imperviousness to vicissitudes that the poet celebrates.

How often have we been told of the irreverent and playful manner Sarojini Naidu adopted towards Mahatma Gandhi. I quote a recent testimony from Shrimati Vijayalakshmi Pandit's autobiography, *The Scope of Happiness:*

"The one person who was really able to help Gandhiji to relax and enjoy a joke was Sarojini Naidu. She was herself a unique human being with a fund of amusing stories and could say that most outrageous things without giving offence. It was she who nicknamed Gandhiji 'Mickey Mouse' when he was at the height of his fame, and he enjoyed this name as much as anyone and asked all sorts of questions about Mickey Mouse, whom he never had seen on the screen. Sarojini was the only one who, so far as I remember, could joke with him on his views of *brahmacharya,* chastity. Once when an article appeared in *Young India* suggesting several ways of avoiding the temptations of females, the writer advised, among other things, the wearing of dark glasses. As C. Rajagopalachari, popularly known as Rajaji and afterwards our first Governor General, always wore very dark glasses, Sarojini would make all kinds of naughty remarks about him, in which both Gandhiji and Rajaji himself would join.

Rajaji's views on the subject were as staunch as Gandhiji's but both put up with Sarojini's merciless teasing. One thing to be remembered and admired is that in those days our leaders could laugh at themselves and at each other, even on matters they considered of great importance. Today, alas, this has become impossible, and the ability to laugh at anything is fast vanishing.

She could talk playfully of Gandhiji's poverty: "you do not know how much it costs us to keep him poor"! Behind all this apparent irreverence was her abiding faith in the quality of grace that Gandhiji brought into the life of this nation. When he died at the hands of a misguided fanatic, her courageous reaction was: "What is all this sniveling about? Would you rather he died of decrepit old age or indigestion? This was the only death great enough for him." Later she wrote: "How and in what lexicon of the world's tongues, shall I find words of adequate beauty and power that might serve, even approximately, to portray the rare and exquisite courtesy and compassion, courage, wisdom, honour and humanity of this unique man who was assuredly the lineal descendant of all the great teachers who taught the gospel of love, Truth and peach for the salvation of humanity, and who was essentially akin to all the saints and prophets, religious reformers and spiritual revolutionaries of all times and lands?" She added: "I love to remember him as the playmate of the children, as the giver of solace to the sorrowful, the oppressed and the fallen. I love to recall the picture of him at his evening prayers facing a multitude of worshippers, with the full moon slowly rising over a silver sea, the very spirit of immemorial India... But perhaps the most poignant and memorable of all is the last picture of him walking to his prayers at the sunset hour on January 30, 1948, translated in a tragic instant of martyrdom from mortality into immortality."

Years earlier, describing Gandhiji's trial in 1922, she had written: "The strange trial proceeded and as I listened to the immortal words that gloved with prophetic fervour from the lips of my beloved master, my thoughts sped across the centuries to a different land and a different age when a similar drama was enacted and another divine and gentle teacher was crucified for spreading a kindred gospel with kindred courage. I realised now that the lowly Jesus of Nazareth, cradled in a manger, furnished the only parallel in history to this invincible apostle of Indian liberty, who loved humanity with unsurpassed compassion, and, to use his own beautiful phrase, 'approached the poor with the mind of the poor,"

I should like to add here another instance of Sarojini Naidu's sense of history. The year was 1947. She had assumed office as Governor of Uttar Pradesh, and she watched the British flag being hauled down for the last time from the flagpost over the Residency at Lucknow. "As I watched the flag coming down," she said, "I wept." I remember reading the text of a B.B.C. broadcast in which the speaker, a British visitor to India, recalled this with a grateful acknowledgement of the spirit in which Sarojini had reached to a historic event.

On the public platform, she was the most enchanting spellbinder in an era of veritable spellbinders. It was the heyday of Indian political oratory. The soul-killing tediousness of the speech-makers we have to put up with these days would give us no idea of the contribution that genuine eloquence made to our freedom movement. Even so, there were people who were suspicious of the rhetoric. As Padmini Sen Gupta reports, "Pandit Motilal Nehru, for instance, was suspicious of excessive emotion in politics. After hearings Sarojini's poetic and impromptu presidential address at Kanpur in 1925, which moved most of the audience to tears, his only comment was: 'But what did she say'? This sent me searching for the text of the address, perhaps the shortest ever delivered by a President of the Indian National Congress. As was her usual practice, she spoke without notes, and by any standard, I find it a most notable performance. It contained a reasoned and impassioned plea for Hindu-Muslim unity, insistence on the need for rescuing the peasantry from their indigence, some wise words on the controversial subject of communal representation and a memorable peroration:

"In the battle of liberty, fear is the one unforgivable treachery and despair the one unforgivable, fear is the one unforgivable treachery and despair the one unforgivable sin. With palms uplifted in ardent supplication, I pray that to us in our coming hour of travail may be granted in sufficient measure an invincipble faith and an inflexiblc courage, and that He in whose name we begin our labours today will in the hour of our triumph keep as humble, and in the beautiful words of our ancient invocation:

> Lead us out of the unreal into the real,
> Out of darkness into the light,
> Out of death into immortality,"

As against Motilal Nehru's suspicion of Sarojini's rhetotic, we have the testimony of Jawaharlal Nehru, as recorded in his Autobiography: "I remember being moved also in those days by a number of eloquent speeches by Sarojini Naidu. It was all nationalism and patriotism and I was a pure nationalist, my vague socialist ideas of college days having sunk into the background".

Those who have heard Sarojini Naidu testify that there was nothing contrived in her speeches for enticing the audience. Her spontaneity was a marvel. A friend of mine told me once of his attending a convocation of Agra University, where Sarojini Naidu was to give the formal address. Talking to the senate members just before the convocation procession formed, Sarojini dismayed everyone by casually exclaiming, "Lord, what am I going to say to these young people"! My friend told me that, despite all the repute of the distinguished guest speaker, his heart sank within him at the prospect of the threatened improvisation. But his dismay was shortlived. Once the speaker started, he was enthralled. He said to me that he had never been thrilled and amused, by turn, as he was that day.

That reminded me of a story of the great actress Ellen Terry who, in a performance of *Merry Wives of Windsor* in a London theatre, suddenly forgot her lines. She was to emerge from under a bed and speak her lines. She emerged all right, but instead of speaking the lines that Shakespeare had written, Ellen Terry turned her beautiful eyes towards heaven and said loudly, "Lord, what shall I do, I've forgotten my lines," The audience roared with delight, and in the tumult, Ellen Terry was able to remember her lines. The perfect rapport that Sarojini was able to establish with her audience was similarly magical. As with Gandhiji and Rajaji, so with any audience in India, she could get away with anything.

I shall end with a rather ribald example. I heard this from another great performer on the platform, Dr. C.V. Raman, who told the story during a scientific lecture on 'Smell and Taste'. He told us that Sarojini was on a visit to South Africa and was being taken round the city of Durban. Suddenly, as they turned into a street, Sarojini stopped and said, "I smell India" the rest of the company presumed that it was some poetic reference to the fragrance of the champak or the jasmine or something of the sort. They were however not left in doubt. Sarojini explained in one word; "Urine!" That was the odour that had assaulted her olfactory nerves. A talent for plain speaking was one of her great gifts. On innumerable occasions, she helped her companions-in-arms to clear their maind of cant. Paraphrasing a well-known line from Wordsworth, we could turn to the spirit of Sarojini Devi and say most fervently, "Thou shouldst be living at this hour!"

PART TWO

GOKHALE THE MAN: A TRIBUTE

by **Sarojini Naidu**

Reprinted from the Bombay Chronicle

I

"I wish I had been anywhere near so that I could have gone to see you personally. I do hope your grief will break into songs that will abide." These beautiful words written on the 12th February, with no apparent premonition of his own fast approaching end, reached me in Calcutta on the sad occasion of my father's *shradh* ceremony. A few days later, Gopal Krishna Gokhale passed away amid the profound sorrow of a nation for once united in the face of an irreparable calamity and loss.

Columns after columns have filled the press with able and eloquent tributes to his manifold and heroic struggles in the cause of India. In every Indian city and remotest centre of Indian interests, men of all creeds and communities, of the most diverse schools of political thought and aspiration, have combined to pay their last offering of reverence and regret for one whose whole life has been a matchless record of selfless devotion to a country for whose welfare he so zealously laboured, in whose dear service he so untimely, so tragically died. And, no poor word of mine is needed to further illumine the story of his noble career or to enhance the value of such universal lamentation and praise. But, I feel, that no chronicle of a great man's work and character can present a complete human document without some of those more personal touches which, however slight and incidental in themselves, may yet act as passing flash-lights to reveal the inmost qualities of his mind. In this short sketch, I shall strive to set down a few of my reminiscences of him, not as Gokhale the politician and social reformer, but simply Gokhale the man, as it was my special privilege to know him in his later years.

A Lovely Comradeship

My personal association with Mr. Gokhale commenced, as it ended, with a written message. It had fallen to me to propose the resolution on the education of women at the Calcutta Sessions of the All-India Social Conference of 1906; and, something in my speech moved him sufficiently to pass me these hurried and cordial sentences which, unworthy as I know myself of such generous appreciation, I venture to transcribe, since they struck the keynote of all our future intercourse. "May I take the liberty," he wrote "to offer you my most respectful and enthusiastic congratulations? Your speech was more than an intellectual treat of the highest order. It was a perfect piece of art. We all felt for the moment to be lifted to a higher plane."

An acquaintance begun on such a happy note of sympathy, grew and ripened at the last into a close and lovely comradeship which I counted among the crowning honours of my life. And, though it was not without its poignant moments of brief and bitter estrangement, our friendship was always radiant both with the joy of spiritual refreshment and the quickening challenge of intellectual discussion and dissent.

Above all, there was the ever-deepening bond of our common love for the motherland; and, for a short space, there was also the added tie of a tender dependence, infinitely touching and childlike, on such comfort and companionship as I, with my own broken health, could render him through long weeks of suffering and distress in a foreign land.

Between 1907 and 1911, it was my good fortune to meet him several times, chiefly during my flying visits to Bombay, but also on different occasions, in Madras, Poona and Delhi. After each meeting I would always carry away the memory of some fervent and stirring words of exhortation to yield my life to the service of India. And, even in the midst of the crowded activities of those epoch-making years, he found leisure to send me now and then, a warm message of approval or encouragement, when any poem or speech or action of mine chanced to please him, or the frequent rumours of my failing health caused him anxiety or alarm.

Paradox of Character

But it was not till the beginning of 1912, when I spent a few weeks in Calcutta with my father, that any real intimacy was established between us. "Hitherto I have always caught you on the wing," he said, "now I will cage you long enough to grasp your true spirit". It was in the course of the long and delightful conversations of this period that I began to comprehend the intrinsic and versatile greatness of the man, and to marvel by what austere and fruitful process he was able to reconcile and assimilate the complex and often conflicting qualities of his essentially dual personality into so supreme an achievement of single-hearted patriotism. It was to me a valuable lesson in human psychology to study the secret of this rich and paradoxical nature. There was the outer man as the world knew and esteemed him, with his precise and brilliant and subtle intellect, his unrivalled gifts of political analysis and synthesis, his flawless and relentless mastery and use of the consummate logic of co-ordinated facts and figures, his courteous but inexorable candour in opposition, his patient dignity and courage in honourable compromise, the breadth and restraint, the vigour and veracity of his far-reaching statesmanship, the lofty simplicities and sacrifices of his daily life. And, breaking through the veils of his many self-repressions, was the inner man that revealed himself to me, in all the intense and urgent hunger of his need for human kinship and affection, in all the intense and urgent hunger of his need for human kinship and affection, in all the tumult and longing, the agony of doubt and ecstacy of faith of the born idealist perpetually seeking some unchanging reality in a world full of shifting disillusion and despair. In him, I felt that both the practical, strenuous worker and the mystic dreamer of dreams were harmonized by the age long discipline of his Brahminical ancestry, which centuries before, had evolved the spirit of the Bhagavad Gita and defined true Yoga as Wisdom in Action. But even he could not escape the limitations of his inheritance. Wide and just as were his recognitions of all human claims to equality, he had nevertheless, hidden away, perhaps unsuspected, something of that conservative pride of his Brahminical descent which instinctively resented the least question of its ancient monopoly of power. One little instance of this weakness—if I may use the word occurs to me. At the All-India Social Conference which was held in Calcutta at the end of 1911, in the course of an address on the so-called Depressed Classes, I happened to have remarked that the denial of their equal human rights and opportunities of life was largely due to the tyranny of arrogant Brahmins in the past. My father who was also present at the meeting, noted and ironically rallied me on the phrase which appealed to both his sense of humour and equity. But, to my surprise, I found that Mr. Gokhale regarded the word "arrogant" almost as a personal affront! "It was no doubt a brave and beautiful speech" he said, in a tone of reproach, "but you sometimes use harsh, bold phrases." Soon after, discussing an allied topic, he burst out saying "You—in spite of yourself—you are typically Hindu in spirit. You begin with a ripple and end in eternity." "But," I answered, a little nettled "when have I ever disclaimed my heritage?"

Another conversation of these weeks stands out with special significance in the light of coming events. One morning, a little despondent and sick at heart about national affairs in general, he suddenly asked me "What is your outlook for India?" "One of hope" I replied. "What is your vision of the immediate future?" "The Hindu-Muslim unity in less than five years" I told him with joyous conviction. "Child" he said, with a note of yearning sadness in his voice, "You are a poet, but you hope too much. It will not come in your lifetime or in mine. But keep you faith and work if you can."

In the March of the following year, I met him for a few minutes only, at a large party in Bombay given by Sir Pherozesha Mehta for the members of the Royal Commission. I had recently brought out a new book of verses which just then, happily for me, was attracting some attention and applause. And Mr. Gokhale's short conversation with me was very characteristic of his attitude of distrust towards such things. "Does the flame still burn brightly?" he questioned. "Brighter than ever," I answered. But he shook his head doubtfully and a little sternly. "I wonder," he murmured, "I wonder how long it will withstand the storm of such excessive adulation and success."

The Privilge of Service for India

A week later, it was my unique privilege to attend and address the now historic sessions of the Muslim League which met in Lucknow on the 22nd March to adopt a new constitution which sounded the keynote of loyal co-operation with the sister community in all matters of national welfare and progress. The unanimous acclamation with which it was carried by both the older and younger schools of Mussalman politicians marked a new era and inaugurated a new standard in the history of modern Indian affairs. From Lucknow I travelled, almost without a break direct to Poona, where I was due on the 25th, and on the morning of the 26th, I walked across with the Honourable Mr. Paranjpye from Fergusson College to the Servants of India Society. I found the world famous leader of the Indian National Congress, weak and suffering from a relapse of his old illness, but busy scanning the journals that were full of comments and criticisms of the Muslim League and its new ideals. "Ah" he cried, with outstretched hands when he saw me, "have you come to tell me that your vision was true?" And he began to question me over and over again with a breathless eagerness that seemed almost impatient of my words, about the real underlying *spirit* of the conference. His weary and pain-wornface lighted up with pleasure when I assured him that, so far at least as the younger men were concerned, it was not an instinct of mere political expediency but one of genuine conviction and a growing consciousness of wider and graver national responsibility that had prompted them to stretch out so frankly and generously, the hand of good fellowship to the Hindus, and I hoped that the coming Congress would respond to it with equal, if not even greater cordiality. "So far as it lies in my power," he answered, "it shall be done."

After an hour or so I found him exhausted with the excitement of the happy news I had brought him from so far; but he insisted on my returning to complete my visit to him that afternoon. When I went back to the Servants of India Society in the evening, I found a strangely transformed Mr. Gokhale, brisk and smiling, a little pale, but without any trace of the morning's languor and depression, "What!" I almost screamed, as he was preparing to lead the way upstairs, "Surely you cannot mean to mount all those steps? You are too ill!" He laughed.

"You have put new hope into me," he said, "I feel strong enough to face life and work again."

Presently his sister and two charming daughters joined us for half an hour on the broad terrace with its peaceful view over sunset hills and valleys, and we talked of pleasant and passing things. This was my first and only glimpse and realisation of the personal domestic side of this lonely and impersonal worker.

After their departure we sat quietly in the gathering twilight till his golden voice, stirred by some deep emotion broke the silence with golden words of counsel and admonition, so grand, so solemn, and so inspiring, that they have never ceased to thrill me. He spoke of the unequalled happiness and privilege of Service for India. "Stand here with me" he said "with the stars and hills for witness and in their presence consecrate your life and your talent, your song and your speech, your thought and your dream to the Motherland. O Poet, see visions from the hill tops and spread abroad the message of hope to the toilers in the valleys."

As I took my leave of him, he said again, to this humble messenger of happy tidings, "You have given me new hope, new faith, new courage. Tonight I shall rest. I shall sleep with a heart at peace."

II

In England

Two months later, early in June, after an absence of fifteen years, I found myself in London once more; and, among the many friends who greeted me on my arrival was the familiar figure of Mr. Gokhale in wholly unfamiliar European garments and—yes—actually an English top hat. I stared at him for a moment. "Where," I asked him "is your rebellious turban?" But I soon got accustomed to this new phase of my old friend, to a social Gokhale who attended parties and frequented theatres, played bridge and entertained ladies at dinner on the terrace of the National Liberal Club—a far cry from the terrace of the Servants of India Society.

In spite of his uncertain health, he was very busy throughout the summer with his work on the Royal Commission and his anxious pre-occupations with Indian affairs in South Africa, then threatening an acute crisis. But he would often come to see me where I was staying at the house of Sir Krishna Gupta. Mr. Gokhale had a great fancy for cherries and I always took care to provide a liberal supply whenever he was expected. "Every man has his price" I would tease him, "and yours is cherries."

One day at the end of July, sitting over a dish of ripe cherries, I broached the subject of a delicate mission which I had undertaken on behalf of the London Indian Association, a new student organisation that had been only a few weeks previously founded by Mr. M. A. Jinnah with the active and eager support of Indian students in London. It was their earnest endeavour to provide a permanent centre to focus the scattered student life in London and to build up such staunch traditions of co-operation and fellowship, that this young association might eventually grow into a perfect miniature and model of the federated India of the future, the India of their dreams; and, it was their ardent desire to start on their new mission of service with a word of sympathy and blessing from this incomparable friend and servant of India.

At first a firm refusal of my request backed by the strict prohibition of his doctors of all undue strain and fatigue somewhat daunted me. But I had a little rashly more or less pledged my word that he would speak, and I redoubled my persuations. "You not only defy all laws of health yourself" he grumbled "but incite me also to disobedience and revolt. Besides"—and his eyes flashed for a moment, "what right had you to pledge your word for me?" "The right" I told him "to demand from you at all costs a message of hope for the young generation."

A few days later, on the 2nd August, he delivered a magnificent inaugural address at Caxton Hall in the presence of a large and enthusiastic audience of students, and set before them those sublime lessons of patriotism and self sacrifice which he alone so signally, among the men of his generation, was competent to teach with authority and grace.

Shortly afterwards he left for India to wage his brave and glorious battle in the cause of his suffering compatriots in South Africa. And though now his health was finally ruined beyond all chance of recovery, it was with the rapture of victorious martyrdom that he wrote from his sick bed, about the end of December, to tell me how prompt and splendid had been the response of a truly united India to the call of her gallant heroes fighting for the eternal laws of right and justice in a far off land.

His Death Warrant

On his return to England in the Spring of 1914, his condition was so precarious as to cause his friends and physicians the gravest concern: and at first he was confined entirely to bed. But with his ever-gracious kindness towards me, he paid me a visit on the very day he was permitted to leave his room, as I was then too ill to go and see him. "Why should a songbird like you have a broken wing," he murmured a little sadly; and presently, he told me that he had just received his own death warrant at the hands of his doctors. With the utmost care; he said, "they think I might perhaps live for three years longer." But, in his calm and thoughtful manner there was no sign of selfish rebellion or fear—only an infinite regret for his unfinished service to India.

Soon, however, I was well enough to accompany him on the short motor drives that were his sole form of recreation; and on mild days, as we sat in the soft sunshine under the budding trees of Kensington Gardens, he would talk to me with that sure instinct of his for choice and graphic phrases that lent his conversation so much distinction and charm. "Give me a corner of your brain that I can call my own," he would say. And in that special corner that was his I treasure many memorable sayings. I learnt to wonder not merely at the range of variety of his culture but at his fastidious preferences for what Charles Lamb has called the delicacies of fine literature. He had too an almost romantic curiosity towards the larger aspects of life and death and destiny and a quick apprehension of the mysterious forces that govern the main springs of human feeling and experience. One day, a little wistfully he said "Do you know, I feel that an abiding sadness underlies all that unfailing brightness of yours. Is it because you have come so near death that its shadows still cling to you?"

"No," I answered "I have come so near life that its fires have burnt me."

But like a homing bird, his heart would always return with swift and certain flight to the one immutable passion of his life, his love for that India, which to him was mistress and mother, goddess and child in one. He would speak of the struggles and disappointments of his early days, the triumphs and failures, the rewards and renunciations of his later years, his vision of India and her ultimate goal, her immediate value as an Imperial asset, her appointed place and purpose in the wider counsels and responsibilities of the Empire.

He spoke too of his work and his colleagues on the Royal Commission, the Viceregal Council and the National Congress; and, though to the end, he remained a better judge of human situations rather than of individuals, I was struck with the essential fairness of his estimates which seemed in one luminous phrase to reveal the true measure of a man. Of one, he said that "He can mould heroes out of common clay" of another that "He has fine sincerity a little marred by hasty judgment," of yet another "He has true stuff in him and that freedom from all sectarian prejudice which will make him the best ambassador of the Hindu-Muslim unity." Of a fourth, "He has made those sacrifices which entitle him to be heard."

Four Leading Questions

Of the many pressing matters that occupied his mind at that time, there were four which to him were of absorbing interest. His scheme for compulsory education which, he felt, was the only solid basis on which to found any lasting national progress. The Hindu-Mussalman question which, he said, could be most fruitfully solved if the leaders of the sister communities would deal in a spirit of perfect unison with certain fundamental problems of equal and urgent importance to both; the high privilege and heavy responsibility of the young generation whose function it was to grapple with more immense and vital issues that his generation had been called upon to face; and of course, the future of the Servants of India Society which was the actual embodiment of all his dreams and devotion for India.

These open-air conversations, however, came to a speedy end. He suddenly grew worse and was forbidden to leave his room or to receive visitors. But, I was fortunate enough to be allowed to see him almost daily for a few hours till his departure to Vichy. In his whimsical way he would call me the best of all his prescriptions. To my usual query on crossing the threshold of his sickroom "Well; am I to be a stimulant or a sedative today?" his invariable reply was "Both". And this one word most adequately summed up the need of his sinking heart and over burdened brain through these anxious and critical weeks.

The interval between his first and second visits to Vichy he spent in a quiet little cottage at Twickenham as the guest and neighbor of Mr. and Mrs. Ratan Tata to whom the nation already owes so many debts of gratitude; and the monotony of the long hours of his temporary and interrupted convalescence was often brightened by the presence of friends whose visits to him were really pilgrimages, and solaced by the devoted attendance of Dr. Jivraj Mehta, who has since won such proud academic honours, and of whom Mr. Gokhale more than once said "He will go far, and be a leader of men."

From Vichy he wrote "Here, in this intense mental solitude. I have come upon the bedrock truths of life and must learn to adjust myself to their demands." The outbreak of war in August brought him back to England a little prematurely. But though his health had obviously improved, and he was better able to stand the strain of his arduous work on the Royal Commission, he seemed oppressed with a sharp and sudden sense of exile in the midst of an alien civilization and people, and to be haunted by a deep nostalgia which he himself could not explain, not merely for the wonted physical scenes and surroundings but for the spiritual texts and tongues of his ancestral land. His conversation during these days was steeped in allusion to the old Sanskrit writers whose mighty music was in his very bold.

The Last Occasion

The last occasion on which I saw him was on the 8th October, two days before I sailed for India. Something, may be, of the autumnal sadness of fallen leaves and growing mists had passed into his mood; or, may be, he felt the fore-shadowing of the wings of Death. But as he bade me farewell, he said, "I do not think we shall meet again. If you live, remember your life is dedicated to the service of the Country. My work is done."

Early in December, shortly after his arrival from Europe, he wrote to complain of the "scurvy trick" fate had played him in a renewal of his 'old trouble' but succeeding letters reported returning strength and ability to work again. In the last letter, written the day before his fatal illness, he spoke of his health being now stationary and of his coming visit to Delhi. But it was otherwise ordained. As the poet says "true as the peach to its ripening taste is destiny to her hour." His predestined hour had already struck. On the 19th February, the selfsame stars that he had invoked two years ago to witness the consecration of a life to the service of India, kept vigil over the passing of this great saint and soldier of the National Righteousness. And of him surely, in another age and in another land were the prophetic words uttered—"Greater love hath no man than this, that a man lay down his life for his friends."

March 5th, 1915.

PART THREE

Sarojini Naidu's Selected Poems

INTRODUCTION

by **Arthur Symons**

It is at my persuasion that these poems are now published. The earliest of them were read to me in London in 1896, when the writer was seventeen; the later ones were sent to me from India in 1904, when she was twenty-five; and they belong, I think, almost wholly to those two periods. As they seemed to me to have an individual beauty of their own, I thought they ought to be published. The writer hesitated. "Your letter made me very proud and very sad," she wrote. "Is it possible that I have written verses that are 'filled with beauty,' and is it possible that you really think them worthy of being given to the world? You know how high my ideal of Art is; and to me my poor casual little poems seem to be less than beautiful—I mean with that final enduring beauty that I desire." And, in another letter, she write: "I am not a poet really. I have the vision and the desire, but not the voice. If I could write just one poem full of beauty and the spirit of greatness, I should be exultantly silent for ever; but I sing just as the birds do, and my songs are as ephemeral." It is for this bird-like quality of song, it seems to me, that they are to be valued. They hint, in a sort of delicately evasive way, at a rare temperament, the temperament of a woman of the East, finding expression through a Western language and under partly Western influences. They do not express the whole of that temperament; but they express, I think, its essence; and there is an Eastern magic in them.

Sarojini Chattopadhyay was born at Hyderabad on February 13, 1879. Her father, Dr. Aghorenath Chattopadhyay, is descended from the ancient family of Chattorajes of Bhramangram, who were noted throughout Eastern Bengal as patrons of Sanskrit learning, and for their practice of Yoga. He took his degree of Doctor of Science at the University of Edinburgh in 1877, and afterwards studied brilliantly at Bonn. On his return to India he founded the Nizam College at Hyderabad, and has since laboured incessantly, and at great personal sacrifice, in the cause of education.

Sarojini was the eldest of a large family, all of whom were taught English at an early age. "I," she writes, "was stubborn and refused to speak it. So one day when I was nine years old my father punished me—the only time I was ever punished—by shutting me in a room alone for a whole day. I came out of it a full-blown linguist. I have never spoken any other language to him, or to my mother, who always speaks to me in Hindustani. I don't think I had any special hankering to write poetry as a little child, though I was of a very fanciful and dreamy nature. My training under my father's eye was of a sternly scientific character. He was determined that I should be a great mathematician or a scientist, but the poetic instinct, which I inherited from him and also from my mother (who wrote some lovely Bengali lyrics in her youth) proved stronger. One day, when I was eleven, I was sighing over a sum in algebra: it *wouldn't* come right; but instead a whole poem came to me suddenly. I wrote it down.

"From that day my 'poetic career' began. At thirteen I wrote a long poem *à la* 'Lady of the Lake'—1300 lines in six days. At thirteen I wrote a drama of 2000 lines, a fullfledged passionate thing that I began on the spur of the moment without forethought, just to spite my doctor who said I was very ill and must not touch a book. My health broke down permanently about this time, and my regular studies being stopped I read voraciously. I suppose the greater part of my reading was done between fourteen and sixteen. I wrote a novel, I wrote fat volumes of journals; I took myself very seriously in those days."

Before she was fifteen the great struggle of her life began. Dr. Govindurajulu Naidu, now her husband, is though of an old and honourable family, not a Brahmin. The difference of caste roused an equal opposition, not only on the side of her family, but of his; and in 1895 she was sent to England, against her will, with a special scholarship from the Nizam. She remained in England, with an interval of travel in Italy, till 1898, studying first at King's College, London, then till her health again broke down, at Girton. She returned to Hyderabad in

September 1898, and in the December of that year, to the scandal of all India, broke through the bonds of caste, and married Dr. Naidu. "Do you know I have some very beautiful poems floating in the air," she wrote to me in 1904; "and if the gods are kind I shall cast my soul like a net and capture them, this year. If the gods are kind—and grant me a little measure of health. It is all I need to make my life perfect, for the very 'Spirit of Delight' that Shelley wrote of dwells in my little home; it is full of the music of birds in the garden and children in the long arched verandah." There are songs about the children in this book; they are called the Lord of Battles, the Sun of Victory, the Lotus-born, and the Jewel of Delight.

"My ancestors for thousands of years," I find written in one of her letters, "have been lovers of the forest and mountain caves, great dreamers, great scholars, great ascetics. My father is a dreamer himself, a great dreamer, a great man whose life has been a magnificent failure. I suppose in the whole of India there are few men whose learning is greater than his, and I don't think there are many men more beloved. He has a great white beard and the profile of Homer, and a laugh that brings the roof down. He has wasted all his money on two great objects: to help other, and on alchemy. He holds huge courts every day in his garden of all the learned men of all religions—Rajahs and beggars and saints and downright villains all delightfully mixed up, and all treated as one. And then his alchemy! Oh dear, night and day the experiments are going on, and every man who brings a new prescription is, you know, only the material counterpart of a poet's craving for Beauty, the eternal Beauty. 'The makers of gold and the makers of verse,' they are the twin creators that sway the world's secret desire for mystery; and what in my father is the genius of curiosity—the very essence of all scientific genius—in me is the desire for beauty. Do you remember Pater's phrase about Leonardo da Vinci, 'curiosity and the desire of beauty'?"

It was the desire of beauty that made her a poet; her "nerves of delight" were always quivering at the contact of beauty. To those who knew her in England, all the life of the tiny figure seemed to concentrate itself in the eyes; they turned towards beauty as the sunflower turns towards the sun, opening wider and wider until one saw nothing but the eyes. She was dressed always in clinging dresses of Eastern silk, and as She was so small, and her long black hair hung straight down her back, you might have taken her for a child. She spoke little, and in a low voice, like gentle music; and she seemed, wherever she was, to be alone.

Through that soul I seemed to touch and take hold upon the East. And first there was the wisdom of the East. I have never known any one who seemed to exist on such "large draughts of intellectual dew" as this child of seventeen, to whom one could tell all one's personal troubles and agitations, as to a wise old woman. In the East, maturity comes early; and this child had already lived through all a women's life. But there was something else, something hardly personal, something which belonged to a consciousness older than the Christian, which I realised, wondered at, and admired, in her passionate tranquility of mind, before which everything mean and trivial and temporary caught fire and burnt away in smoke. Her body was never without suffering, or her heart without conflict; but neither the body's weakness nor the heart's violence could disturb that fixed contemplation, as of Buddha on his lotus-throne.

And along with this wisdom, as of age or of the age of a race, there was what I can hardly call less than an agony of sensation. Pain or pleasure transported her, and the whole of pain or pleasure might be held in a flower's cup or the imagined frown of a friend. It was never found in those things which to others seemed things of importance. At the age of twelve she passed the Matriculation of the Madras University, and awoke to find herself famous throughout India. "Honestly," she said to me, "I was not pleased; such things did not appeal to me." But here, in a letter from Hyderabad, bidding one "share a March morning" with her, there is, at the mere contact of the sun, this outburst: "Come and share my exquisite March morning with me: this sumptuous blaze of gold and sapphire sky; these scarlet lilies that adorn the sunshine; the voluptuous scents of neem and champak and serisha that beat upon the languid air with their implacable sweetness; the thousand little gold and blue and silver breasted birds bursting with the shrill ecstasy of life in nesting time. All is hot and fierce and passionate, ardent and unashamed in its exulting and importunate desire for life and love. And, do you know that the scarlet lilies are woven petal by petal from my heart's blood, these little quivering birds are my soul made incarnate music, these heavy perfumes are my emotions dissolved into aerial essence, this flaming blue and gold sky is the 'very me,' that part of me that incessantly and insolently, yes, and a little deliberately, triumphs over that other part—a thing of nerves and tissues that suffers and cries out, and that must die tomorrow perhaps, or twenty years hence."

Then there was her humour, which was part of her strange wisdom, and was always awake and on the watch. In all her letters, written in exquisite English prose, but with an ardent imagery and a vehement sincerity of emotion which make them, like the poems, indeed almost more directly, un-English, Oriental, there was always this intellectual, critical sense of humour, which could laugh at one's own enthusiasm as frankly as that enthusiasm had been set down. And partly the humour, like the delicate reserve of her manner, was a mask or a shelter. "I have taught myself," she writes to me from India, "to be commonplace and like everybody else superficially. Every one thinks I am so nice and cheerful, so 'brave,' all the banal things that are so comfortable to be. My mother knows me only as 'such a tranquil child, but so strong willed.' A tranquil child!" And she writes again, with deeper significance: "I too have learnt the subtle philosophy of living from moment to moment. Yes, it is a subtle philosophy, though it appears merely an epicurean doctrine: 'Eat, drink, and be merry, for tomorrow we die.' I have gone through so many yesterdays when I strove with Death that I have realised to its full the wisdom of that sentence; and it is to me not merely a figure of speech, but a literal fact. Any tomorrow I might die. It is scarcely two months since I came back from the grave: is it worth while to be anything but radiantly glad? Of all things that life or perhaps my temperament has given me I prize the gift of laughter as beyond price."

Her desire, always, was to be "a wild free thing of the air like the birds, with a song in my heart." A spirit of too much fire in too frail a body, it was rarely that her desire was fully granted. But in Italy she found what she could not find in England, and from Italy her letters are radiant.

"This Italy is made of gold," she writes from Florence, "the gold of dawn and daylight, the gold of the stars, and, now dancing in weird enchanting rhythms through this magic month of May, the gold of fireflies in the perfumed darkness—'aerial gold.' I long to catch the subtle music of their fairy dances and make a poem with a rhythm like the quick irregular wild flash of their sudden movements. Would it not be wonderful? One black night I stood in a garden with fireflies in my hair like darting restless stars caught in a mesh of darkness. It gave me a strange sensation, as if I were not human at all, but an elfin spirit. I wonder why these little things move me so deeply? It is because I have a most 'unbalanced intellect,' I suppose." Then, looking out on Florence, she crise, "God! How beautiful it is, and how glad I am that I am alive today!" And she tells me that she is drinking in the beauty like wine, "wine, golden and scented, and shining, fit for the gods; and the gods have drunk it, the dead gods of Etruria, two thousand years ago. Did I say dead? No, for the gods are immortal, and one might still find them loitering in some solitary dell on the grey hillsides of Fiesole. Have I seen them? Yes, looking with dreaming eyes, I have found them sitting under the olives, in their grave, strong, antique beauty—Etruscan gods!"

In Italy she watches the faces of the monks, and at one moment longs to attain to their peace by renunciation, longs for Nirvana; "then, when one comes out again into the hot sunshine that warms one's blood, and sees the eager hurrying faces of men and women in the street, dramatic faces over which the disturbing experiences of life have passed and left their symbols, one's heart thrills up into one's throat. No, no, no, a thousand times no! How can one deliberately renounce this coloured, unquiet, fiery human life of the earth?"And, all the time, her subtle criticism is alert, and this woman of the East marvels at the women of the West, "the beautiful worldly women of the West," whom she sees walking in the Cascine, "taking the air so consciously attractive in their brilliant toilettes, in the brilliant coquetry of their manner!" She finds them "a little incomprehensible," profound artists in all the subtle intricacies of fascination," and asks if these "incalculable frivolities and vanities and coquetries and caprices" are asks if these "incalculable frivolities and vanities and coquetries and caprices" are, to us, an essential part of their charm? And she watches them with amusement as they flutter about her, petting her as if she were a nice child, a child or a toy, not dreaming that she is saying to herself sorrowfully: "How utterly empty their lives must be of all spiritual beauty their lives must be of all spiritual beauty if they are nothing more than they appear to be."

She sat in our midst, and judged us, and few knew what was passing behind that face "like an awakening soul," to use one of her own epithets. Her eyes were like deep pools, and you seemed to fall through them into depths below depths.

Selected Poems

INDIAN LOVE-SONG

She

Like a serpent to the calling voice of flutes,
Glides my heart into thy fingers, O my Love!
Where the night-wind, like a lover, leans above
His jasmine-gardens and sirisha-bowers;
And on ripe boughs of many-coloured fruits
Bright parrots cluster like vermilion flowers.

He

Like the perfume in the petals of a rose,
Hides thy heart within my bosom, O my love!
Like a garland, like a jewel, like a dove
That hangs its nest in the asoka-tree.
Lie still, O love, until the morning sows
Her tents of gold on fields of ivory.

CRADLE-SONG

From groves of spice,
O'er fields of rice,
Athwart the lotus-stream,
I bring for you,
Aglint with dew
A little lovely dream.

Sweet, shut your eyes,
The wild fire-flies
Dance through the fairy neem;
From the poppy-bole
For you I stole
A little lovely dream.

Dear eyes, good-night,
In golden light
The stars around you gleam;
On you I press
With soft caress
A little lovely dream.

SUTTEE

Lamp of my life, the lips of Death
Hath blown thee out with their sudden breath;
Naught shall revive thy vanished spark...
Love, must I dwell in the living dark?

Thee of my life, Death's cruel foot
Hath crushed thee down to thy hidden root;
Nought shall restore thy glory fled...
Shall the blossom live when the tree is dead?

Life of my life, Death's bitter sword
Hath severed us like a broken word,
Rent us in twain who are but one...
Shall the flesh survive when the soul is gone?

SONG OF A DREAM

Once in the dream of a night I stood
Lone in the light of a magical wood,
Soul-deep in visions that poppy-like-sprang;
And spirits of Truth were the birds that sang,
And spirits of Love were the stars that glowed,
And spirits of Peace were the streams that flowed
In that magical wood in the land of sleep.

Lone in the light of that magical grove,
I felt the stars of the spirits of Love
Gather and gleam round my delicate youth,
And I heard the song of the spirits of Truth,
To quench my longing I bent me low
By the streams of the spirits of Peace that flow
In that magical wood in the land of sleep.

HUMAYUN TO ZOBEIDA

(From the Urdu)

You flaunt your beauty in the rose, your glory in the dawn,
Your sweetness in the nightingale, your whiteness in the swan.

You haunt my waking like a dream, my slumber like a moon,
Pervade me like a musky scent, possess me like a tune.

Yet, when I crave of you, my sweet, one tender moment's grace,
You cry, "I sit behind the veil, I cannot show my face."

Shall any foolish veil divide my longing from my bliss?
Shall any fragile curtain hide your beauty from my kiss?

What war is this of Thee and Me? Give o'er the wanton strife,
You are the heart within my heart, the life within my life.

AUTUMN SONG

Like a joy on the heart of a sorrow,
The sunset hangs on a cloud;
A golden storm of glittering sheaves,
Of fair and frail and fluttering leaves,
The wild wind blows in a cloud.

Hark to a voice that is calling
To my heart in the voice of the wind:
My heart is weary and sad and alone,
For its dreams like the fluttering leaves have gone,
And why should I stay behind?

ALABASTER

Like this alabaster box whose art
Is frail as a cassia-flower, is my heart,
Carven with delicate dreams and wrought
With many a subtle and exquisite thought.

Therein I treasure the spice and scent
Of rich and passionate memories blent
Like odours of cinnamon, sandal and clove,
Of song and sorrow and life and love.

ECSTASY

Cover mine eyes, O my Love!
Mine eyes that are weary of bliss
As of light that is poignant and strong
O silence my lips with a kiss,
My lips that are weary of song!

Shelter my soul, O my love!
My soul is bent low with the pain
And the burden of love, like the grace
Of a flower that is smitten with rain:
O shelter my soul from thy face!

TO MY FAIRY FANCIES

Nay, no longer I may hold you,
In my spirit's soft caresses,
Nor like lotus-leaves enfold you
In the tangles of my treasses
Fairy fancies, fly away
To the white cloud-wildernesses,
Fly away!

Nay, no longer ye may linger
With your laughter-lighted faces,
Now I am a thought worn singer
In life's high and lonely places.
Fairy fancies, fly away,
To bright wind inwoven spaces,
Fly away!

MY DEAD DREAM

Have you found me, at last, O my Dream? Seven æons ago
You died and I buried you deep under forests of snow.
Why have you come hither? Who bade you awake from your sleep
And track me beyond the cerulean foam of the deep?

Would you tear from my lintels these sacred green garlands of leaves?
Would you scare the white, nested, wild pigeons of joy from my eaves?
Would you touch and defile with dead fingers the robes of my priest?
Would you weave your dim moan with the chantings of love at my feast?
Go back to your grave, O my Dream, under forests of snow,
Where a heart-riven child hid you once, seven æons ago.
Who bade you arise from your darkness? I bid you depart!
Profane not the shrines I have raised in the clefts of my heart.

DAMAYANTE TO NALA IN THE HOUR OF EXILE

(A fragment)

Shalt thou be conquered of a human fate,
My liege, my lover, whose imperial head
Hath never bent in sorrow of defeat?
Shalt thou be vanquished, whose imperial feet
Have shattered armies and stamped empires dead?

Who shall unking thee, husband of a queen?
Wear thou thy majesty inviolate.
Earth's glories flee of human eyes unseen,
Earth's kingdoms fade to a remembered dream,
But thine henceforth shall be a power supreme,
Dazzling command and rich dominion,
The winds thy heralds and thy vassals all
The silver-belted planets and the sun.
Where'er the radiance of thy coming fall,
Shall dawn for thee her saffron footcloths spread,
Sunset her purple canopies and red,
In serried splendour, and the night unfold
Her velvet darkness wrought with starry gold
For kingly raiment, soft as cygnet down.
My hair shall braid thy temples like a crown
Of sapphires, and my kiss upon thy brows
Like cithar-music lull thee to repose,
Till the sun yield thee homage of his light.

O king, thy kingdom who from thee can wrest?
What fate shall dare uncrown thee from this breast,
O god-born lover, whom my love doth gird
And armour with impregnable delight
Of Hope's triumphant keen flame-carven sword?

THE QUEEN'S RIVAL

I

Queen Gulnaar sat on her ivory bed,
Around her countless treasures were spread;

Her chamber walls were richly inlaid
With agate, porphory, onyx and jade;

The tissues that veiled her delicate breast,
Glowed with the hues of a lapwing's crest;

But still she gazed in her mirror and sighed:
"O King, my heart is unsatisfied."

King Feroz bent from his ebony seat:
"Is thy least desire unfulfilled, O Sweet?

"Let thy mouth speak and my life be spent
To clear the sky of thy discontent."

"With none to envy and none gainsay,
No savour or salt hath my dream or day."

Queen Gulnaar sighed like a murmuring rose:
"Give me a rival, O King Feroz."

II

King Feroz spoke to his Chief Vizier:
"Lo! ere to-morrow's dawn be here,

"Send forth my messengers over the sea,
To seek seven beautiful brides for me;

"Radiant of feature and regal of mien,
Seven handmaids meet for the Persian Queen."

Seven new moon tides at the Vesper call,
King Feroz led to Queen Gulnaar's hall.

A young queen eyed like the morning star:
"I bring thee a rival, O Queen Gulnaar."

But still she gazed in her mirror and sighed:
"O King, my heart is unsatisfied."

Seven queens shone round her ivory bed,
Like seven soft gems on a silken thread,

Like seven fair lamps in a royal tower,
Like seven bright petals of Beauty's flower.

Queen Gulnaar sighed like a murmuring rose:
"Where is my rival, O King Feroz?"

III

When spring winds wakened the mountain floods,
And kindled the flame of the tulip buds,

When bees grew loud and the days grew long,
And the peach groves thrilled to the oriole's song,

Queen Gulnaar sat on her ivory bed,
Decking with jewels her exquisite head;

And still she gazed in her mirror and sighed:
"O King, my heart is unsatisfied."

Queen Gulnaar's daughter two spring times old,
In blue robes bordered with tassels of gold,

Ran to her knee like a wildwood fay,
And plucked from her hand the mirror away.

Quickly she set on her own light curls
Her mother's fillet with fringes of pearls;

Quickly she turned with a child's caprice
And pressed on the mirror a swift, glad kiss.
Queen Gulnaar laughed like a tremulous rose:
"Here is my rival, O King Feroz."

THE POET TO DEATH

Tarry a while, O Death, I cannot die
While yet my sweet life burgeons with its spring;
Fair is my youth, and rich the echoing boughs
Where dhadikulas sing.

Tarry a while, O Death, I cannot die
With all my blossoming hopes unharvested,
My joys ungarnered, all my songs unsung,
And all my tears unshed.

Tarry a while, till I am satisfied
Of love and grief, of earth and altering sky;
Till all my human hungers are fulfilled,
O Death, I cannot die!

THE INDIAN GIPSY

Is tattered robes that board a glittering trace
Of bygone colours, broidered to the knee,
Behold her, daughter of a wandering race,
Tameless, with the bold falcon's agile grace,
And the lithe tiger's sinuous majesty.

With frugal skill her simple wants she tends,
She folds her tawny heifers and her sheep
On lonely meadows when the daylight ends,
Ere the quick night upon her flock descends
Like a black panther from the caves of sleep.

Time's river winds in foaming centuries
Its changing, swift, irrevocable course
To far off and incalculable seas;
She is twin-born with primal mysteries,
And drinks of life at Time's forgotten source.

Jaya Surya, œtat 4

Golden sun of victory, born
In my life's unclouded morn,
In my lambent sky of love,
May your growing glory prove
Sacred to your consecration,
To my heart and to my nation.
Sun of victory, may you be
Sun of song and liberty.

Padmaja, œtat 3

Lotus-maiden, you who claim
All the sweetness of your name,
Lakshmi, fortune's queen, defend you,
Lotus-born like you, and send you
Balmy moons of love to bless you,
Gentle joy-winds to caress you.
Lotus-maiden, may you be
Fragrant of all ecstasy.

Ranadheera, œtat 2

Little lord of battle, hail
In your newly-tempered mail!
Learn to conquer, learn to fight
In the foremost flanks of right,
Like Valmiki's heroes bold,
Rubies girt in epic gold.
Lord of battle, may you be,
Lord of love and chivalry.

Lilamani, œtat 1

Limpid jewel of delight
Severed from the tender night
Of your sheltering mother-mine,
Leap and sparkle, dance and shine,
Blithely and securely set
In love's magic coronet.
Living jewel, may you be
Laughter-bound and sorrow-free.

THE PARDAH NASHIN

Her life is a revolving dream
Of languid and sequestered ease;
Her girdles and her fillets gleam
Like changing fires on sunset seas;
Her raiment is like morning mist,
Shot opal, gold and amethyst.

From thieving light of eyes impure,
From coveting sun or wind's caress,
Her days are guarded and secure
Behind her carven lattices,
Like jewels in a turbaned crest,
Like secrets in a lover's breast.

But though no hand unsanctioned dares
Unveil the mysteries of her grace,
Time lifts the curtain unawares,
And Sorrow looks into her face...
Who shall prevent the subtle years,
Or shield a woman's eyes from tears?

TO YOUTH

O Youth, sweet comrade Youth, wouldst thou be gone?
Long have we dwelt together, thou and I;
Together drunk of many an alien dawn,
And plucked the fruit of many an alien sky.

Ah, fickle friend, must I, who yesterday
Dreamed forwards to long, undimmed ecstasy,
Henceforward dream, because thou wilt not stay,
Backward to transient pleasure and to thee?

I give thee back thy false, ephemeral vow;
But, O beloved comrade, ere we part,
Upon my mournful eyelids and my brow
Kiss me who hold thine image in my heart.

NIGHTFALL IN THE CITY OF HYDERABAD

See how the speckled sky burns like a pigeon's throat,
Jewelled with embers of opal and peridote.

See the white river that flashes and scintillates,
Curved like a tusk from the mouth of the city-gates.

Hark, from the minaret, how the muezzin's call
Floats like a battle-flag over the city wall.

From trellised balconies, languid and luminous
Faces gleam, veiled in a splendor voluminous.

Leisurely elephants wind through the winding lanes,
Swinging their silver bells hung from their silver chains.

Round the high Char Minar sounds of gay cavalcades
Blend with the music of cymbals and screnades.

Over the city bridge Night comes majestical,
Borne like a queen to a sumptuous festival.

STREET CRIES

When dawn's first cymbals beat upon the sky,
Rousing the world to labour's various cry,
To tend the flock, to bind the mellowing grains,
From ardent toil to forge a little gain,
And fasting men go forth on hurrying feet,
Buy bread, buy bread, rings down the eager street.

When the earth falters and the waters swoon
With the implacable radiance of noon,
And in dim shelters koils hush their notes,
And the faint, thirsting blood in languid throats
Craves liquid succor from the cruel heat,
Buy fruit, buy fruit, steals down the panting street.

When twilight twinkling o'er the gay bazaars,
Unfurls a sudden canopy of stars,
When lutes are strung and fragrant torches lit
On white roof-terraces where lovers sit Drinking together
of life's poignant sweet,
Buy flowers, buy flowers, floats down the singing street.

TO INDIA

O young through all thy immemorial years!
Rise, Mother, rise, regenerate from thy gloom,
And, like a bride high-mated with the spheres,
Beget new glories from thine ageless womb!

The nations that in fettered darkness weep
Crave thee to lead them where great mornings break…
Mother, O Mother, wherefore dost thou sleep?
Arise and answer for thy children's sake!

Thy Future calls thee with a manifold sound
To crescent honours, splendours, victories vast;
Waken, O slumbering Mother and be crowned,
Who once wert empress of the sovereign Past.

THE ROYAL TOMBS OF GOLCONDA

I Muse among these silent fanes
Whose spacious darkness guards your dust;
Around me sleep the hoary plains
That hold your ancient wars in trust.
I pause, my dreaming spirit hears,
Across the wind's unquiet tides
The glimmering music of your spears,
The laughter of your royal brides.

In vain, O Kings, doth time aspire
To make your names oblivion's sport,
While yonder hill wears like a tiar
The ruined grandeur of your fort.

Though centuries falter and decline,
Your proven strongholds shall remain
Embodied memories of your line,
Incarnate legends of your reign.

O Queens, in vain old Fate decreed
Your flower-like bodies to the tomb;
Death is in truth the vital seed
Of your imperishable bloom
Each new-born year the bulbuls sing
Their songs of your renascent loves;
Your beauty wakens with the spring
To kindle these pomegranate groves.

TO A BUDDHA SEATED ON A LOTUS

Lord Buddha, on the Lotus-throne,
With praying eyes and hands elate,
What mystic rapture dost thou own,
Immutable and ultimate?
What peace, unravished of our ken,
Annihilate from the world of men?

The wind of change for ever blows
Across the tumult of our way,
To-morrow's unborn griefs depose
The sorrows of our yesterday.
Dream yields to dream, strife follows strife,
And Death unweaves the webs of Life.

For us the travail and the heat,
The broken secrets of our pride,
The strenuous lessons of defeat,
The flower deferred, the fruit denied;
But not the peace, supremely won,
Lord Buddha, of thy Lotus-throne.

With futile hands we seek to gain
Our inaccessible desire,
Diviner summits to attain,
With faith that sinks and feet that tire;
But nought shall conquer or control
The heavenward hunger of our soul.

The end, elusive and afar,
Still lures us with its beckoning flight,
And all our mortal moments are
A session of the Infinite.
How shall we reach the great, unknown
Nirvana of thy Lotus-throne?

SELECTED FOLK SONGS

PALANQUIN-BEARERS

Lightly, O lightly we bear her along,
She sways like flower in the wind of our song;
She skims like a bird on the foam of a stream,
She floats like a laugh from the lips of a dream.
Gaily, O gaily we glide and we sing,
We bear her along like a pearl on a string.

Softly, O softly we bear her along,
She hangs like a star in the dew of our song;
She springs like a beam on the brow of the tide,
She falls like a tear from the eyes of a bride.
Lightly, O lightly we glide and we sing,
We bear her along like a pearl on a string.

WANDERING SINGERS

(Written to one of their Tunes)

Where the voice of the wind calls our wandering feet,
Through echoing forest and echoing street,
With lutes in our hands ever singing we roam,
All men are our kindred, the world is our home.

Our lays are of cities whose luster is shed,
The laughter and beauty of women long dead;
The sword of old battles, the crown of old kings,
And happy and simple and sorrowful things.
What hope shall we gather, what dreams shall we sow?
Where the wind calls our wandering footsteps we go.
No love bids us tarry, no joy bids us wait:
The voice of the wind is the voice of our fate.

INDIAN WEAVERS

Weavers, weaving at break of day,
Why do you weave a garment so gay?...
Blue as the wing of a halcyon wild,
We weave the robes of a new-born child.

Weavers, weaving at fall of night,
Why do you weave a garment so bright?...
Like the plumes of a peacock, purple and green,
We weave the marriage-veils of a queen.

Weavers, weaving solemn and still,
What do you weave in the moonlight chill?...
White as a feather and white as a cloud,
We weave a dead man's funeral shroud.

CORAMANDEL FISHERS

Rist, brothers, rise, the wakening shies pray to the
morning light,
The wind lies asleep in the arms of the dawn like a child
that has cried all night.
Come, let us gather our nets from the shore, and set our
catamaraus free.
To capture the leaping wealth of the tide, for we are
the sons of the sea.

No longer delay, let us hasten away in the track of the sea gull's call,
The sea is our mother, the cloud is our brother, the waves
are our comrades all
What though we toss at the fall of the sun where the hand
of the sea-god drives?
He who holds the storm by the hair, will hide in his
breast our lives.

Sweet is the shade of the coconut glade, and the scent
of the mango grove,
And sweet are the sands at the full o' the moon with
the sound of the voices we love.
But sweeter, O brothers, the kiss of the spray and
the dance of the wild foam's glee:
Row, brothers, row to the blue of the verge, where
the low sky mates with the sea.

THE SNAKE-CHARMER

Whither dost thou hide from the magic of my flute-call?
In what moonlight-tangled meshes of perfume,
Where the clustering keovas guard the squirrel's slumber,
Where the deep woods glimmer with the jasmine's bloom?

I'll feed thee, O beloved, on milk and wild red honey,
I'll bear thee in a basket of rushes, green and white,
To a palace-bower where golden-vested maidens
Thread with mellow laughter the petals of delight.

Whither dost thou loiter, by what murmuring hollows,
Where oleanders scatter their ambrosial fire?
Come, thou subtle bride of my mellifluous wooing,
Come, thou silver-breasted moonbeam of desire!

CORN-GRINDERS

O little mouse, why dost thou cry
While merry stars laugh in the sky?

Alas ! Alas ! My lord is dead!
Ah, who will ease my bitter pain?
He went to seek a millet-grain
In the rich farmer's granary shed;
They caught him in a baited snare,
And slew my lover unaware:
Alas! Alas! My lord is dead.

O little deer, why dost thou moan,
Hid in thy forest-bower alone?

Alas! Alas! My lord is dead
Ah! Who will quiet my lament?
At fall of eventide he went
To drink beside the river-head;
A waiting hunter threw his dart,
And struck my lover through the heart:
Alas! Alas! My lord is dead.

O little bride, why dost thou weep
With all the happy world asleep?
Alas! Alas! My lord is dead!
Ah, who will stay these hungry tears,
Or still the want of famished years,
And crown with love my marriage-bed?
My soul burns with the quenchless fire That lit my lover's
funeral pyre:
Alas! Alas! My lord is dead.

VILLAGE-SONG

Honey, child, honey, child, whither are you going?
Would you cast your jewels all to the breezes blowing?
Would you leave the mother who on golden grain has fed you?
Would you grieve the lover who is riding forth to wed you?

Mother mine, to the wild forest I am going,
Where upon the champa boughs the champa buds are blowing;
To the koil-haunted river-isles where lotus lilies glisten,
The voices of the fairy-folk are calling me:
O listen!

Honey, child, honey, child, the world is full of pleasure,
Of bridal-songs and cradle-songs and sandal-scented leisure.
Your bridal robes are in the loom, silver and saffron glowing,
Your bridal cakes are on the hearth: O whither are you going?

The bridal-songs and cradle-songs have cadences of sorrow,
The laughter of the sun to-day, the wind of death to-morrow.
For sweeter sound the forest-notes where forest-streams are
falling;
O mother mine, I cannot stay, the fairy-folk are calling.

IN PRAISE OF HENNA

A kokila called from a henna-spray:
Lira! Liree! Lira! Liree!
Hasten, maidens, hasten away
To gather the leaves of the henna-tree.
Send your pitchers afloat on the tide,
Gather the leaves ere the dawn be old,
Grind them in mortars of amber and gold,
The fresh green leaves of the henna-tree.

A kokila called from a henna-spray:
Lira! Liree! Lira! Liree!
Hasten maidens, hasten away
To gather the leaves of the henna-tree.
The tilka's red for the brow of a bride,
And betel-but's red for lips that are sweet;
But, for lily-like fingers and feet,
The red, the red of the henna tree.

HARVEST HYMN

Men's Voices

Lord of the lotus, lord of the harvest,
Bright and munificent lord of the morn!
Thine is the bounty that prospered our sowings,
Thine is the bounty that nurtured our corn.
We bring thee our songs and our garlands for tribute,
The gold of our fields and the gold of our fruit;
O giver of mellowing radiance, we hail thee,
We praise thee, O Surya, with cymbal and flute.

Lord of the rainbow, lord of the harvest,
Great and beneficent lord of the main!
Thine is the mercy that cherished our furrows,
Thine is the mercy that fostered our grain.
We bring thee our thanks and our garlands for tribute,
The wealth of our valleys, new-garnered and ripe;
O sender of rain the dewfall, we hail thee,
We praise thee, Varuna, with cymbal and pipe.

Women's Voices

Queen of the gourd flower, queen of the harvest,
Sweet and omnipotent mother, O Earth!
Thine is the plentiful bosom that feeds us,
Thine is the womb where our riches have birth.
We bring thee our love and our garlands for tribute,
With gifts of thy opulent giving we come;
O source of our manifold gladness, we hail thee,
We praise thee, O Prithvi, with cymbal and drum.

All Voices

Lord of the Universe, Lord of our being,
Father eternal, ineffable Om!
Thou art the Seed and the Scythe of our harvests,
Thou art our Hands and our Heart and our Home.
We bring thee our lives and our labours for tribute,
Grant us thy succor, thy counsel, thy care.
O Life of all life and all blessing, we hail thee,
We praise thee, O Bramha, with cymbal and prayer.
Manor Lodgenal

PART FOUR

Sarojini Naidu's Selected Letters 1896-1911

Manor Lodge
Frognal
July, 1896

Dear Tessa,

Thank you. I shall be delighted to look in on you on Sunday, to say goodbye before I go to my 'matter of fact' but 'very good-for-you' life in Cambridge!

I have just come back from Egham after a most beautiful time in the Windsor woods—

'Vague with autumn's golden mystery'

When a silly thing came into my head, only two lines of which have anything to do with the woods, the rest is to be almost an ill-behaved person who went wandering all over to find peace. I believe, and at last came across it somewhere in a musty old ward where sat a superannuated sage! I have only done the last two verses, and I am most disgusted with myself!

Will you give your father the verses I enclose and make him promise not to be too severe on me when I come on Sunday.

I am, Dear Tessa,
Yours very affectionately
Sarojini Chattopadhyay

P.S. I had a longer letter from the 'Keats of Ohio', and she sends all sorts of sweet messages to your parents—for conveying which, I shall expect an extra lump of sugar on Sunday!

Manor Lodge.
[illegible]

Dear Tessa, Thank you. I shall be delighted to look in on Sunday, to say good-bye before I go to my 'matter-of-fact' but 'very-good-for-you' life in Cambridge!

I have just come back from Egham after a most beautiful time in the Windsor woods 'Vague with autumn's golden mystery', where a silly thing came into my head only [illegible] of which have anything to do with the woods, though it is rather about an ill-behaved person who went wandering all over, to find Peace I believe, & at last came across in a musty old room where sat a superannuated Sage! I have only done the last two verses, I am most disgusted with myself! Will you give your father the verses

I enclose, and make him promise not to be too severe on me when I come on Sunday.

I am, Dear Tessa,
Yours very affectionately
Sarojini Chattopâdhyây

P.S.
I had a longer letter from the 'Keats of Ohio', and she sends all sorts of sweet messages to your parents — for conveying which, I shall expect an extra lump of sugar on Sunday!

Lullaby for Sunalini

Where the golden-glowing
Champak-buds are blowing
By the silver-flowing streams,
Into where Day is dying,
There are fairies flying,
Scattering a cloud of dreams.

II

Slumber-spirits winging
Thro' the forest singing,
Flutter hither bringing, soon,
Baby-visions sleeping
For my Sunalini —
Hush thee, mother's pretty Moon!

III

Sweet the Saints shall bless thee —
Hush, mine arms caress thee,
Hush my heart I do press thee, sleep!
Till the red Dawn dances
Breaking thy soft trances,
Sleepy Sunalini, sleep!

June

I

I am a child of the Night and of wild desolations,
I am a Spirit of glittering starlight and tears,
Mine is the dower of the dreams of a shadowed nation,
Mine is a crown of the ashes of numberless years.

II

You are a son of the splendours of love and of glory,
These are the garlands of Dawn round your beautiful head,
Yours is the light of the new-risen ages of story,
Mine is the gloom of the land of an age that is dead.

III

Yours is the music of hope and the joy of tomorrow,
Yours is a sky that no legend of old hath become (?),
Mine is a song that is broken with echoes of sorrow,
Haunted with moans of the wraiths from the mystical Past!

July 1896

Serenade

[illegible]he green lies a musical breeze
[illegible]ters and flits on invisible wing
[illegible]amaranth dells by the slumber-deep wells
[illegible]e jackals are silent, the Kokilas sing
[illegible]n the amethyst-hush of the meadows of Night
Sweet thoughts like a fragrance of [illegible]
And the magical stars in a murmur of light,
Dreamily, drowsily, faintly spring.

II

Come to me, Sweet, on silver-swift feet,
Awake thee, awake from thine exquisite dreams,
I await thee, I wait, O love thou art late,
I await thee, I wait, by the wandering stream,
O come with a kiss on thy lotus-lips' bloom,
And strangle my soul in thy tresses' perfume,
O come to me, love, like a moon in the gloom,
Awake thee, awake from thine exquisite dream!

June 96.

Serenade

Thro' the green trees a musical breeze
Flutters and flits on invisible wing,
In amaranth dells by the slumber – deep wells
The jackals are silent, the kokhilas sing
In the amethyst hush of the meadows of Night
Sweet thoughts like a fragrance of roses take flight,
and the magical stars in a murmur of light,
Dreamily, drowsily, fairily spring.

II

Come to me, sweet, on silver-swift feet,
Awake thee, awake from thine exquisite dream,
I await thee, I wait, O love, thou art late,
I wait thee, I wait, by the wandering stream,
O come with a kiss on thy lotus-lips' bloom,
And strangle my soul in thy tresses' perfume,
O come to me,
Love, 'like a moon in the gloom,
Awake thee, awake from thine exquisite dream!

June '96

Lullaby for Sunalini

Where the garden-glowing
Champak buds are blowing
By the silver-flowing streams,
now when Day is dying,
There are fairies flying,
Scattering a cloud of dreams.

II

Slumber spirits winging
Thro' the forest singing
Flutter hither bringing, some

Baby visions shiny
For my Sunalini
Hush thee, mother's pretty Moon!

III

Sweet the Saints shall bless thee
Hush, mine arms caress Thee,
Hush my heart doth press thee, sleep!
Till the red Dawn dances
Breaking thy soft trances,
Sleep my Sunalini, sleep!

June '96

I

I am a child of the night and of mild desolation
I am a spirit of glittering starlight and tears
Mine is the dander of the dreams of a shadow-bound nation,
Mine is a crown of the ashes of numberless years.

II

You are a son of the splendour of love and of glory
These are the garlands of dawn around your
Beautiful head,
Yours is the light of the new-risen ages of story,
Thine is the gloom of the land of an age that is dead.

III

Yours is the music of hope and the joy of tomorrow,
Yours is the sky that no legend of old hath forecast
Thine is a song that is broken with echoes of sorrow,
Haunted with moans of the wraiths from the mystical past!

July 1896

Manor Lodge
Frognal
21st Sept 1896

Dear Mr Gosse,

I don't think these recourses of mine will interest you very much. They are only personal things sincerely felt and badly expressed. The one I rather like myself is 'Right on the Rhine'.

You found me in a 'down in my luck' mood last night. It's because my one desire is to be not with the many who have talent , but with the few who have genius, and I know it is as impossible as it is conceited!

However, if you think there is anything more in me than the mere facility and the spontaneous impulse which I trust I possess, of course I must go on writing and hoping to do something someday.

And I have filled a whole page with myself which it is not exactly what is called modest, but the ending of my letter shall be most charming, because it ends with a thousand kind and hearty birthday wishes from

Yours most sincerely,
Sarojini Chattopadhyay

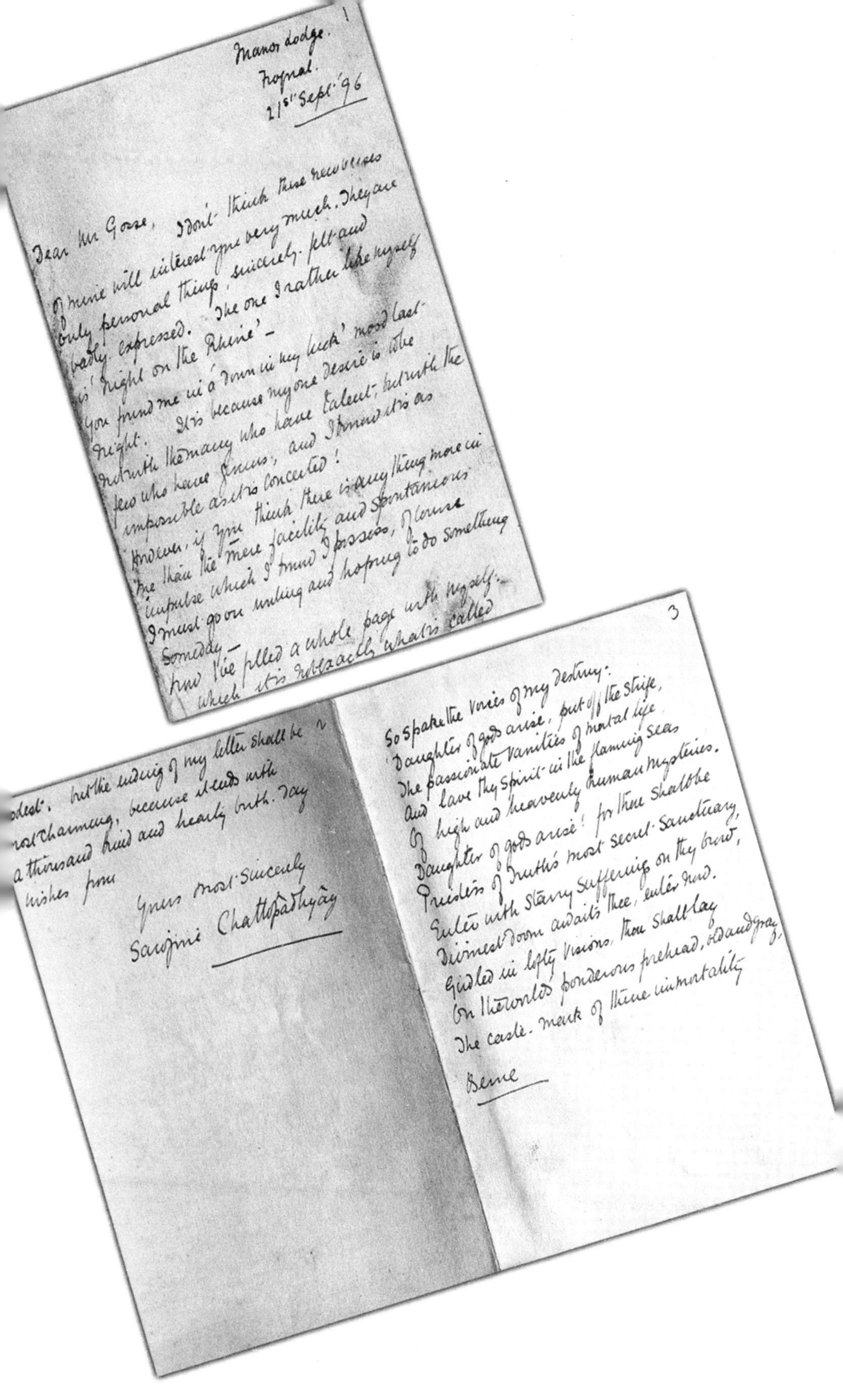
Manor Lodge.
Nopnal.
21st Sept. '96

Dear Mr Gosse, I don't think these new verses of mine will interest you very much. They are only personal things, sincerely felt and badly expressed. The one I rather like myself is 'Night on the Rhine' —

You found me in a 'down in my luck' mood last night. It's because my one desire is to be not with the many who have talent, but with the few who have genius; and I know it's as impossible as it is conceited!

However, if you think there is anything more in me than the mere facility and spontaneous impulse which I know I possess, of course I must go on writing and hoping to do something someday —

Now I've filled a whole page with myself, which it is not exactly what is called modest. But the ending of my letter shall be most charming, because it ends with a thousand kind and hearty birth-day wishes from

Yours most sincerely
Sarojini Chattopadhyay

So spake the voices of my destiny:
'Daughter of gods arise, put off the strife,
The passionate vanities of mortal life,
And lave thy spirit in the flaming seas
Of high and heavenly human mysteries.
Daughter of gods arise! for thee shall be
Priestess of Truth's most secret sanctuary,
Enter with starry suffering on thy brow,
Divinest doom awaits thee, enter now.
Girdled in lofty visions, thou shalt lay
On the world's ponderous forehead, old and gray,
The caste-mark of thine immortality'

Berne

So spake the voices of my destiny:
Daughter of gods arise, put off the strife
The passionate vanities of mortal life
And love thy spirit in the flaming seas
Daughter of gods arise! For thee shall be
Priestess of Truth's most secret sanctuary
Enter with starry sufferings on thy brow
Dimmest doom awaits thee, enter now
Girdled in lofty visions thou shall lay
On the world's ponderous forehead, old and gray
The caste mark of thine immortality
Serve.

Manor Lodge
Frogn al
28th September 1896

Dear Tessa,

A tiny song came into my head yesterday, quite suddenly as if it dropped from the wind: it isn't great poetry you know, but I think it is rather pretty and, I wish to make it prettier still by dedicating it to you. Will you accept it from me in token of all that I feel for a certain 'sunset blessed maiden'—and believe me, dear Tessa,

Affectionately yours,
Sarojini Chattopadhyay

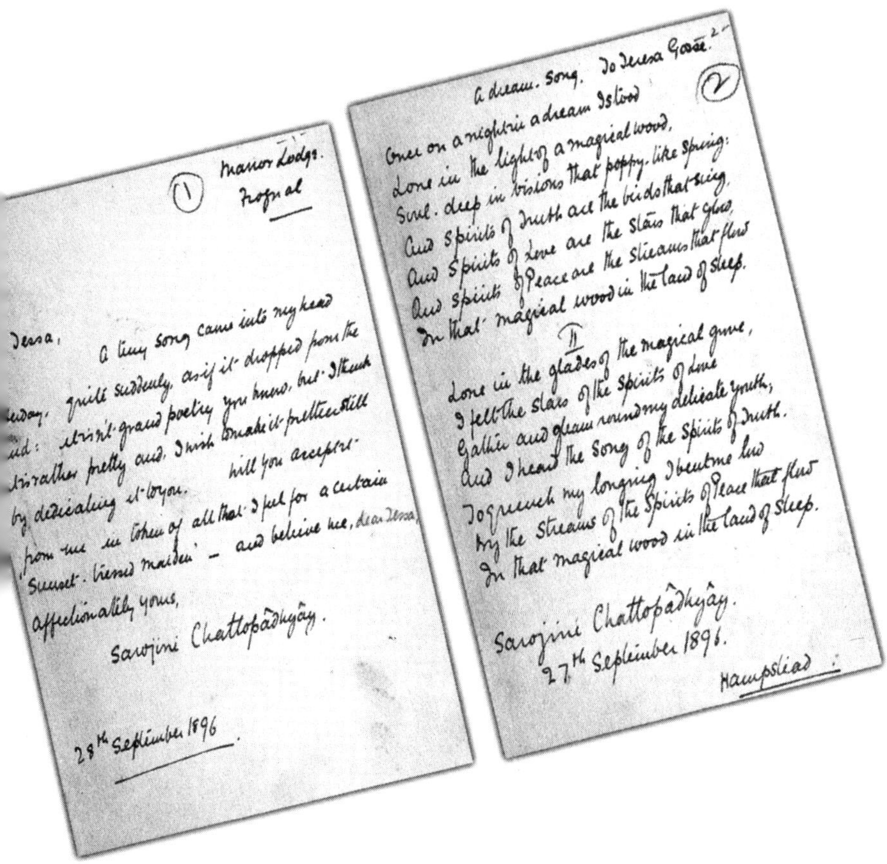
1
Manor Lodge.
Frognal

Tessa,
A tiny song came into my head
...erday, quite suddenly, as if it dropped from the
...d: it isn't great poetry you know, but I think
...is rather pretty and I wish to make it prettier still
by dedicating it to you. Will you accept
from me in token of all that I feel for a certain
sunset-blessed maiden' – and believe me, dear Tessa,
affectionately yours,
Sarojini Chattopadhyay.

28th September 1896.

2
A dream. Song. To Tessa Gosse.

Once on a night in a dream I stood
Lone in the light of a magical wood,
Soul-deep in visions that poppy-like spring:
And spirits of Truth are the birds that sing,
And spirits of Love are the stars that glow,
And spirits of Peace are the streams that flow
In that magical wood in the land of sleep.

II

Lone in the glades of the magical grove,
I felt the stars of the spirits of Love
Gather and gleam round my delicate youth,
And I heard the song of the spirits of Truth.
To quench my longing I bent me low
By the streams of the spirits of Peace that flow
In that magical wood in the land of sleep.

Sarojini Chattopadhyay.
27th September 1896.
Hampstead.

A dream song To Teresa Gosse

Once on a night in a dream I stood
Lone in the light of a magical wood,
Soul deep in visions that poppy-like spring
And spirits of truth are the birds that sing
And spirits of love are the stars that glow,
And spirits of Peace are the streams that flow
In that magical wood in the land of sleep.

II

Lone in the glades of the magical grove
I felt the stars of the spirits of love
Gather and gleam round my delicate youth,
And I heard the song of the spirits of truth
To quench my longing I bent down low
By the streams of the spirits of peace that flow
In that magical wood in the land of sleep.

Sarojini Chattopadhyay
27th September 1896
Hampstead

Manor Lodge,
Monday

Dear Mr Gosse,

As Mr Harland remarked yesterday, your "harshness" is worth more to me than the smiles (literary) of other critics. So I am sending you four new things I have lately written.

The Serenade and the Lullaby are mere experiments in eastern rhythms – the first of Persian, the second of Bengalee.

The Eastern Dancers, which I think Mr Symons wants to print in the Savoy was suggested by his "Javanese Dancers". I have chosen that long full metre to try and give something of the voluptuous movements of the dancers.

The other poem, or should I say "verses"—has only just come into my head—I wonder if there is much sense in it.

You see it was rash of you to let me make you my "task-master". I trouble you far too often don't I? But you are so kind and I do hope your coat isn't spoilt!

Very sincerely yours
Sarojini Chattopadhyay

Last night as we were pursuing a cab, Mr Yeats with his mystic eyes glowing star like in the dark, and his sepulchral voice sounding very solemn asked me—if I ever saw visions!

1

Mannsdodge.
Maunt
Hampstead
N.W.

Monday

Dear Mr Gosse, As Mr Harland remarked yesterday, your "harshness" is worth more to me than the smiles (literary) of other critics — so I am sending you four new things I have lately written.

The Serenade and the Lullaby are mere experiments in Eastern rhythms — the first of Persian, the second of Bengalee.

The Eastern Dancers, which I think Mr Symons wants to print in the Savoy, was suggested by his "Javanese Dancers" — I have chosen that long, full metre to try & give something of the voluptuous movements of the dancers.

The other poem, or should I say "verses" — has only just come into my head — & I wonder if there is much sense in it —

You see it was rash of you to let me make you my "task-master" — I trouble you far too often don't I? — but you are so kind — & I do hope your coat isn't spoilt!

Very Sincerely yours,

Sarojini Chattopadhyay

Last night as we were pursuing a cab, Mr Yeats with his mystic eyes glowing star-like in the dark, & his sepulchral voice sounding very solemn asked me — if I ever saw visions!

35 Blomfield Road
Maisa Hill
Oct 6 1896

Dear Mr Gosse,

I do not dare to trust myself to thank you for what you said on Sunday. You cannot know what those words meant to me, how they will always colour my life, how, when I am in the very depths of self disgust and despair as I so often am, they will give me new hope and new courage—no, you cannot know!

Poetry is the one thing I love so passionately, so intensely, so absolutely that is my very life of life—and now you have told me that I am a poet—*I am a poet*! I keep repeating it to myself to try to realise it. Will you let me tell you a little about myself, because I want you to know how you have been an influence in my life-ever since I was eleven years old!

Beautiful and romantic and remarkable as were the circumstances amidst which I was brought up, there was nothing to directly encourage poetry—Indeed, the strongest influences that were brought to bear upon us were scientific and mathematical. I always loved poetry but nothing could be further from my mind than trying to write verses myself—it never once occurred to me why—till one day, when I was about eleven, while I was trying to do a dull problem, algebra it was I think, quite suddenly three verses came into my head and I wrote them down. Of course they were worthless, but that day marked a new era in my life. I was going to be a poet. I did not tell anyone about my new 'adventures', but went on writing things began to come with real ease and rapidity —weak and childish no doubt—I have no records left! And somehow my father got hold of them and soon everybody got to know and I was of course the most marvellous thing in creation and everything I did henceforth was wonderful, divine, etc. I was faulty, on the way where my head turned with all that flood of success but remarkably blind and injudicious praise and flattery. About this time, I don't know how or why the name of Edmund Gosse began to be a sort of magical legend to me. Legends were more real than realities then and in a dim, vague kind of way, I began to feel that somehow this magical name was to be one of the strongest and most inevitable influences on my life.

I went on writing and Hyderabad began to feel more and more mad about what I did; indeed, I think really all over India I began to be looked on as a phenomenon, but the more they praised, the more disgusted I got with myself and longed passionately for somebody who could really criticise. I knew my verses were very poor, but I wanted to know if they had even a germ of promise of better things to come. At last in despair I wrote you a letter (it must have been very childish I suppose; this was when I was about fourteen or fifteen) but I burnt it the next day!

Then I had a long and terrible illness which nearly killed me and I believe for a time nearly half paralysed my faculties—everything seemed gone, except the love of poetry and the longing to do better. Then I came to England. I was about sixteen. I must have been singularly ignorant for sixteen because I know England to me meant Shelly and Keats who were dead and Edmund Gosse who was alive and certainly made up by far the greater part of England! (I think Westminster Abbey and the Thames made up the rest!) Well, I made up my mind that I must know Edmund Gosse! For the past six months I did not, could not write a single line or indeed do anything and then suddenly the fountains were unsealed and I began to write, write, write! In three months I wrote I think nearly 45 pieces—horrible! But the verses had,. I thought less strength than some of my earlier one's—the first batch I sent you were selections from this exuberant outburst of bad verse!

Well, in January I first saw you, the magical legend had become a reality and I was not disappointed—indeed I shall never forget that day because with one great step I seemed to wake into a new, large life, the life I had always longed for and so long in vain. From that day I seemed an altered being. I seemed to have put off childish things and put on the garments of a new and beautiful hope and ambition, and I have gone on growing and growing. I feel it—seeing more clearly, feeling more intensely, thinking more deeply and loving more passionately, more unselfishly that beautiful spirit of Art that has now become dearer than my life's blood to me, and all this I owe to you. I know I have not expressed myself at all well but you will understand me, I think, and you will not mind me telling you all this.

As you have so long been so good an influence in my life, I want you to go on forever! I will send you everything I write and you must tell me what you think. I want you to be more severe and exacting than ever, the better I do because I do not want to outlast the years, but the centuries. That is very conceited of me, but is it not worthwhile to aim at the stars, though one never gets beyond a mountain top? I don't think I am going to ask you to excuse me for taking up so much of your time. Because I cannot go on being grateful to you in silence without your knowing how much cause I have to be grateful to you for! Ever believe me.

Yours in all gratitude,
Sarojini Chattopadhyay

My most humble respects to Charles Nathaniel

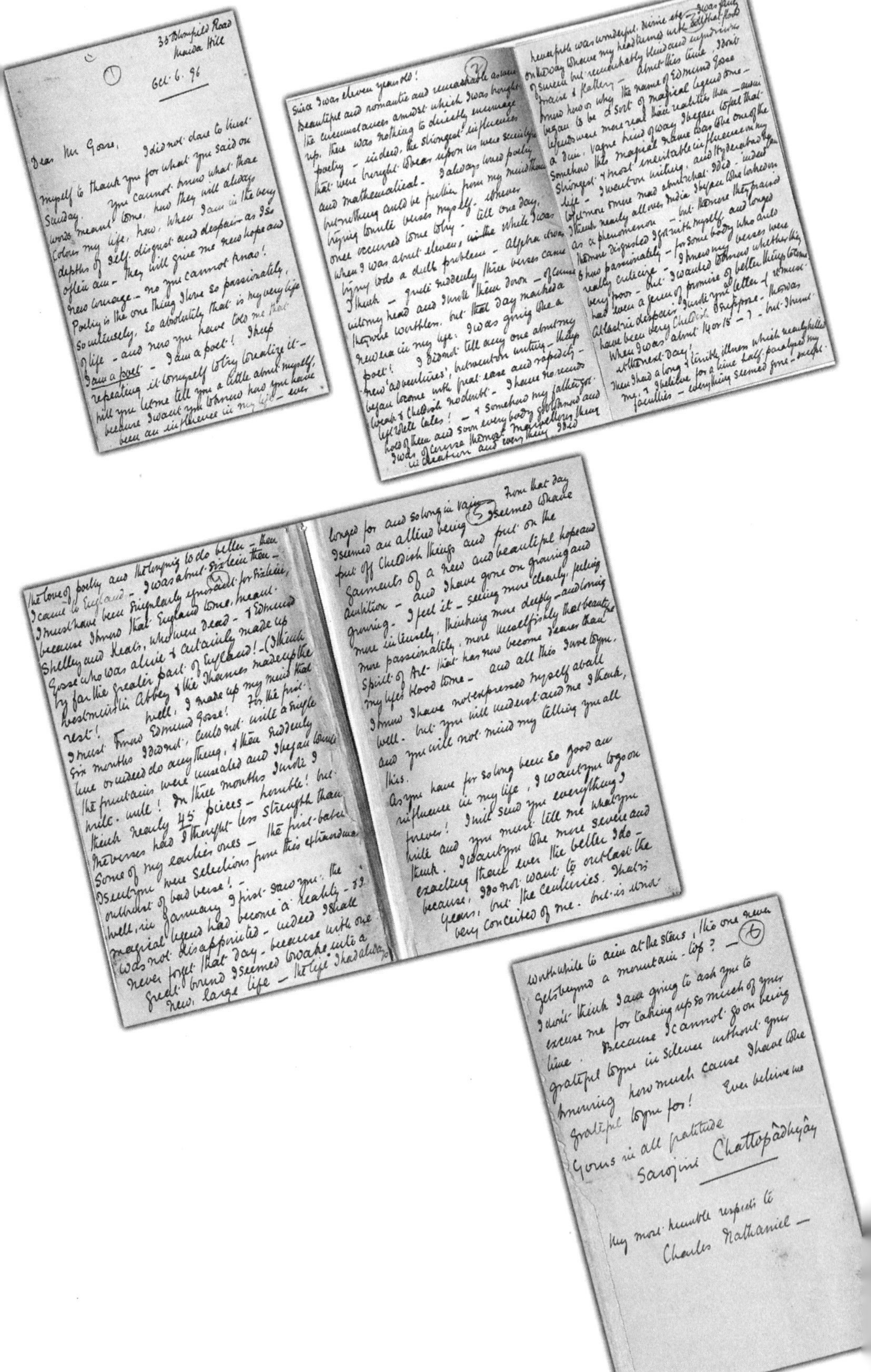

33 Blomfield Road
Maida Hill
Oct. 6. 96

Dear Mr Gosse, I did not dare to trust myself to thank you for what you said on Sunday. You cannot know what those words meant to me, how they will always colour my life, how, when I am in the very depths of self-disgust and despair as I so often am — they will give me new hope and new courage — no you cannot know! Poetry is the one thing I love so passionately, so intensely, so absolutely that it is my very life of life — and now you have told me that I am a poet — I am a poet! I keep repeating it to myself to try to realize it — will you let me tell you a little about myself, because I want you to know how you have been an influence in my life — ever since I was eleven years old!

Beautiful and romantic and remarkable as were the circumstances amidst which I was brought up, there was nothing to directly encourage poetry — indeed, the strongest influences that were brought to bear upon us were scientific and mathematical. I always loved poetry but nothing could be further from my mind than trying to write verses myself. However once it occurred to me why — till one day, when I was about eleven, while I was trying to do a dull problem — Algebra it was I think — quite suddenly three verses came into my head and I wrote them down — of course they were worthless, but that day marked a new era in my life: I was going to be a poet! I did not tell any one about my new 'adventures', but went on writing — they began to come with great ease and rapidity — weak & childish no doubt — I have no record left of these tales! — & somehow my father got hold of them and soon everybody got to know and I was of course thought marvellous, their ... in creation and everything I did henceforth was wonderful. Since then — I was fairly on the way to where my head turned with all that flood of sweet but remarkably blind and unmerited praise & flattery — About this time, I don't know how or why, the name of Edmund Gosse began to be a sort of magical legend to me — legends were more real than realities then — and in a dim, vague kind of way I began to feel that somehow this magical name was to be one of the strongest & most inevitable influences in my life — I went on writing, and Hyderabad began to feel more & more proud about what I did — indeed I think nearly all over India I began to be looked on as a phenomenon — but the more they praised the more disgusted I got with myself, and longed so passionately — for somebody who could really criticise — I knew my verses were very poor — but I wanted to know whether they had even a germ of promise of better things to come. At last in despair I wrote you a letter (I must have been very childish I suppose — then — I was about 14 or 15 —) — but I burnt it the next day! Then I had a long & terrible illness which nearly killed me, & I believe for a time half paralysed my faculties — everything seemed gone — except the love of poetry and the longing to do better — then I came to England — I was about sixteen then — I must have been singularly ignorant for sixteen, because I knew that England to me, meant Shelley and Keats, who were dead — & Edmund Gosse who was alive & certainly made up by far the greater part of England! — (I think Westminster Abbey & the Thames made up the rest!) Well, I made up my mind that I must know Edmund Gosse! For the first six months I did not, could not write a single line or indeed do anything, & then suddenly the fountains were unsealed and I began to write. write! In three months I wrote I think nearly 45 pieces — horrible! but the verses had I thought less strength than some of my earlier ones — The first batch I sent you were selections from this extraordinary outburst of bad verse! — Well, in January I first saw you: the magical legend had become a reality — I was not disappointed — indeed I shall never forget that day — because with one great bound I seemed to wake into a new, large life — the life I had always longed for and so long in vain. From that day I seemed to have — I seemed an altered being and put off childish things and put on the garments of a new and beautiful hope and ambition — and I have gone on growing and growing. I feel it — seeing more clearly, feeling more intensely, thinking more deeply — and loving more passionately, more unselfishly that beautiful Spirit of Art — that has now become dearer than my life's blood to me — and all this I owe to you. I know I have not expressed myself at all well — but you will understand me I think, and you will not mind my telling you all this.

As you have for so long been so good an influence in my life, I want you to go on forever! I will send you everything I write and you must tell me what you think. I want you to be more severe and exacting than ever the better I do — because, I do not want to outlast the years, but the centuries. That is very conceited of me — but is it not worth while to aim at the stars, if one never gets beyond a mountain-top? — I don't think I am going to ask you to excuse me for taking up so much of your time. Because I cannot go on being grateful to you in silence without your knowing how much cause I have to be grateful to you for! Ever believe me

Yours in all gratitude
Sarojini Chattopâdhyây

My most humble respects to Charles Nathaniel —

Girton College
Cambridge
10th Nov 1896

Dear good task master,

May I write to you? I am sending you one or two things I've written since I've been here. They are somewhat disappointing, but the spirit of poetry is thwarted in this place of too much intellectuality.

You have seen Girton and you know the permanent part of it, which consists of the building, the grounds, and last but not the least the dons, who, though 'girls may come and girls may go,' still go on forever. There is little else I can tell or rather I have no right to utter what are I suppose unpardonable heresies. I have a theory that most things depend more or less on the 'point of view', but there seems something very wrong with my 'point of view'. This is a place for people who are gifted with strong and distinct brain and muscular power, for a girl must either be clever or athletic, very often both to be a true Girtonian or to really enjoy Girton life, which of course is made up of difficult books and exciting games. But there are some temperaments that care passionately for the vivid and vital things of life, for dear-bought experiences and deep thought and keen emotions and for them, Girton is certainly not an ideal place of education, unless of course education means one part convention by which all natures are to be reduced to one soulless and uninteresting pattern! Save me from education!

In the effort to lead at once two separate lives that are essentially at war with each other, the one that is inevitably a part of my very soul and the other a life, no I will not call it life, but all existence that has to be tested and accepted and existed. I have rather broken down turned very weary and very despondent. They seem to cramp each other, hurt each other constantly these two irreversibly entwined lives of mine! What shall I do with them, can you tell me?

I daren't ask you what new work you are doing; but I hope you are intending to publish something quite soon; it is more than six months since you gave us some of your strong refreshing work, the broad, keen vitality and thoughtfulness of which are so absolutely reviving after much of the latter day 'productions' of clever authors: they seem to have such a cheap if distinctly brilliant knack of saying clever and 'alert' things, it seems to me; which while seeming deep, have very little more than surface—depth!

How is Mrs Gosse now? I hope she doesn't suffer very much pain. Please give her my love and tell her I mean to sound her a little when I come 'down'. I am going to write to Tessa soon. I don't in the least appreciate the portrait she has sent, nor the 'extracts from a sweet versifier'. By the way, I wonder why the younger poets have been doing so little, if any of really fine work; work in which the series of infinite 'prettiness fancy' have no part!

Have you good news of the two wanderers? I suppose Sylvia will be back soon—*so* French!

Need I make a long and polite apology for writing this letter? But, on second thoughts I won't, for I have enjoyed writing to you my good 'task-master'! Goodbye.

With all due respect to his feline majesty Charles Nathaniel,

I remain,
Ever yours sincerely
Sarojini Chattopadhyay

(1)

Girton College
Cambridge.
10th Nov: '96

Dear "good task-master",

May I write to you?

I am sending you one or two things I've written since I've been here: they are somewhat disappointing; but the Spirit of Poetry is thwarted in this place of too much intellectuality.

You have seen Girton; and you know the permanent part of it, which consists of the building, the grounds, and last, but not least, the Dons, who, though "girls may come and girls may go, still go on for ever" —

There is little else I can tell, or rather, I have no right to utter what are I suppose unpardonable heresies. I have a theory that most things depend more or less on the point of view; but there seems something very wrong with my "point of view" —

This is a place for people who are gifted with strong and distinct brain and muscular power; for a girl must either be clever or athletic, very often both, to be a true Girtonian, or to really enjoy

(2)

Girton life which of course is made up of difficult text-books and exciting games. But there are some temperaments that care passionately for the vivid and vital things of life; for keen emotions; and for deep thought and clear bright experiences; and for them, Girton is certainly not an ideal place of education, unless of course, education means one great convention by which all natures are to be reduced to one sullen and uninteresting pattern! Save me from education!

In the effort to lead, at once, two separate lives that are essentially at war with each other — the one that is inevitably a part of ~~my~~ very soul, and the other a life, no I will not call it life, but an existence that has to be tolerated and accepted and existed — ~~one~~ I have rather broken down from very weary and very despondent. They seem to cramp each other, hurt each other constantly — these two irreconciably-natured lives of mine! What shall I do with them, can you tell me?

(3)

I daren't ask you what new work you are doing, but I hope you are intending to publish something quite soon; it's more than six months since you gave us some of your strong refreshing work, the broad, keen vitality and thoughtfulness of which are so absolutely reviving after ~~the~~ much of the latter-day productions of "clever" authors: they seem to have such a cheap if distinctly brilliant knack of saying clever and "alert" things, it seems to me, which while seeming deep, have very little more than surface-depth!

How is Mrs Gosse now? I hope she doesn't suffer very much pain — please give her my love, and tell her I mean to borrow her a little when I come "down" — I am going to write to Tessa soon; I don't in the least appreciate the portrait she has sent, nor the "extracts from a Sweet Versifier". By the way I wonder why the "younger poets" have been doing so little, if any, of really fine work; with which the sins of their finite prettiness

(4)

[the]y have no part!

[Hav]e you good news of the two wanderers — I suppose [S]ylvia will be back soon, so French!

[N]eed I make a long and "polite" apology for [wr]iting this letter? but, on second thoughts I won't, for I have enjoyed writing to you, my "good task-master" —

Good bye. With all due respects to his Gelic majesty Charles Nathaniel,

I remain,

Ever yours, sincerely,

Sarojini Chattopadhyay

Wellington Complex SI West
Eastburne May 6, 1897

Dear Mr. Gosse,

Here's something quite new for you. Prose!

This little sketch came suddenly into my head yesterday and I wrote it down – there is nothing in it I know, but I want you to tell me if you think it is worthwhile for me to try to write prose.

It seems to me that prose has a far greater influence than poetry and the best way to reveal India to England is through prose.

I have scarcely tried anything in the shape of a story because I can never make a plot. But if you think my prose is not altogether hopeless, I should like to practice writing. I have such loads of material for stories.

This little sketch is a quite probable incident and it is really, a great deal of it from life. Will you send it back to me if it is a failure?

I am longing to see you all again, but I don't think I shall be back in London before the end of this month.

It will be glorious to get better and be able to do some work. When one is ill it seems almost impossible to do anything good, unless one is Robert Louis Stevenson or Mrs Browning!

You are very disappointed in me, aren't you? But, will you wait a little while before you give me up for a fraud?

I mean to do very good work someday if you will believe in me- and I shall dedicate what you think the very best to you.

My love to everyone.

Yours affectionately
Sarojini Chattopadhyay

P.S. I have enjoyed your XVII century studies so much.

15

(1)

Wellington Crompton St. West.
Eastbourne. May 6. 1897.

Dear Mr Gosse, Here's something quite new for you –
prose!
This little sketch came suddenly into my head yesterday
and I wrote it down – there is nothing in it I know,
but I want you to tell me if you think it is worth while
for me to try to write prose.
It seems to me prose has a far greater influence
than poetry and the best way to reveal India
to England is through prose.
I have scarcely tried anything in the shape of a story,
because I can never make a plot. But if you
think my prose isn't altogether hopeless,
I should like to practise writing. I have such
worlds of material for stories.
This little sketch is a quite probable incident –

(2)

it is really, a great deal of it from life –
Will you send it back to me if it is a failure?

I am longing to see you all again, but I
don't think I shall be back in London before
the end of this month.
It will be glorious to get better and be able to do
some work. When one is ill it seems almost
impossible to do anything good, unless one
is Robert Louis Stevenson or Mrs Browning!
You are very disappointed in me, aren't you?
But, will you wait a little while before you
give me up for a pound?
I mean to do very good work someday if you
will believe in me – and I shall dedicate
what you think the very best to you.

My love to every one.
Yours affectionately
Sarojini Chattopadhyay.

(3)

P.S.
I have enjoyed your XVII Century Studies so
much.

Hyderabad Deccan
August 1899

My dear and honoured literary sponsor, I send you a greeting!

I must forego the delights of your birthday supper, the witty talk more sparkling and exhilarating than the birthday champagne. But I can still have the pleasure of sending you a birthday greeting?

I am sending an ivory paper knife. I wish it to be symbolical. The knife itself of the keen pleasure of so genuine a book lover in cutting open the pages of a new book; and the exquisite workmanship to denote your preferences for the delicacies of true literature.

I am writing from my bed, which seems to have become my permanent 'citadel'. But I console myself on my bodily afflictions with the profound and amazing philosophy of Epictetus.

From my childhood I have felt a strange irresistible hunger for the study of philosophy but so long I have always curbed my desire, knowing myself too young, too weak to wander in peril through all those bewildering and sinuous mazes of thought, the mysteries of infinite contradictions, subtleties, doubts....

Doubt! It is the keynote of all philosophy. What's doubt but the passion ate cry of the soul in its supreme necessity for faith?

The old passion is upon me once more and demands fulfilment with a more imperious accent. Well! I am twenty (in my arrogance of youth it seems a great age to me, as doubtless it seemed once to you also!) I feel I have a clue that will eventually bring me over safely home from the alluring and dangerous labyrinth! So I have given myself over to the old philosophies. Come upon a sage in the rapture of absolute self

Incarnation of a prayer
That has overcome the strife
Of the passing things of life

A true spiritual descendent of the great Rishis, who shall keep something of their 'fallen day' about him. But otherwise it is merely a marvellous, fantastic, physical world where everything revolves itself into material situations. Sensuous enjoyments, infinitely picturesque and pleasant to the artistic sense, like a representation of some old eastern fairytale on the stage, but on this modern world of actualities the restless change and conflict, the perpetual hurrying onwards to the fulfilment of new destinies, new creeds. Hyderabad seems another unreality as detached and illusive as a day dream.

You recollect those lines
'Built Nineveh with our sighing,
And Babylon itself in our mirth'

Had the poet even dreamed of this city he had substituted Hyderabad for Babylon.....

Someday you must come here and let me pay back in ever so slight a measure, the generous and delightful hospitality I received at your hands. Probably before then we shall fly northward with the summer birds and claim a double measure of your kindness—the gods hasten that dear day!

Salaam alekum! Peace be on you, O genuine soul and genial hearted scholar, dreaming in the benign shadow of your bronze victory.

Your affectionate Indian godchild
Sarojini Naidu

Mrs Gosse is supposed to read a whole letter to herself between the lines of this whose wisdom, whose knowledge so limited!

Greek philosophy, all 'the glory that was Greece' but the radiant flower that had the immemorial wisdom of the East for its roots: roots that sprang and were nurtured from the very core of eternal things.

Like Gaulier, I am one for whom the visible world exists... this definite, dramatic world of so varied and fiery beauty, colour, music, perfume and vivid human faces. It is this deeply inherent instruct for a concrete and tangible world that effectually connects and balances my eastern birthright of mysticism, the ever strengthening tendency and yearning to merge myself and become part of the Abstract Universal Essence. Poets collect the eternal Beauty, Philosophers, the Ultimate wisdom. Lovers the immortal love and the rest name it God.

I carry your last words to me as a sort of talisman, a prophesy as well as a blessing: 'May you write beautiful poems'.

I have written nothing yet but it is not you who will reprove me for my deliberate silence. In one of your letters to me, letters that I treasure, you bade me as an 'image of golden bronze for the God to speak thro'.

Yes, I wait for the moment of ecstasy when the accents of the god are unmistakable. Many things vaguely strike me, craving utterance. But I dare not speak like speech is invaluable and utters itself......

What an egotistical letter to send you!

But why should not my literary sponsor be also father confessor to my literary faiths?

There is no news of literary interest to send you of Hyderabad. There is intellectual life here, no ardent vital 'movement'.....here and there, it is true in some remote forest-dell or secluded hillside.

[Hy]derabad Deccan
August 1899

My dear and honoured literary Sponsor. I send you a greeting!

I must forego the delight of your birth-day supper, the witty talk more sparkling and exhilarating than the birth-day champagne: but I can still have the pleasure of sending you a birth-day greeting.

I am sending an ivory paper-knife. I wish it to be symbolical. The knife itself of the keen pleasure of so genuine a book-lover in cutting open the pages of a new book, and the exquisite workmanship to denote your preferences for the 'delicacies of fine literature'.

I am writing from my bed, which seems to have become my permanent 'citadel'. but I console myself for my bodily afflictions with the profound and amusing philosophy of Epictetus.

(2)

[Fro]m my childhood I have felt a strange, irresistible hunger for the study of philosophy, but so long I have always curbed my desire, knowing myself too young, too weak to wander in their perilous paths through all those bewildering and sinuous mazes of thought, the mysteries of infinite contradictions, subtleties, doubt...

Doubt: is the keynote of all philosophy. And what is Doubt but the passionate cry of the soul in its supreme necessity for faith?

The old passion surprises me once more and demands fulfilment with a more imperious accent. Well! I am twenty (it may be arrogance of youth: seems a great age to me, as doubtless it [illegible] once to you also!) — I feel I have [illegible] a clue that will eventually bring me out safely from the alluring and dangerous labyrinths. So I have given myself over to the old philosophers.

(3)

Come upon a day, in the rapture of absolute self abnega[tion]
like a rare
Incarnation of a prayer
That has overcome the strife
Of the passing hungers of life'.

While spiritual descendant of the great Rishis, she still keeps something of their '[illegible] day' about her. But otherwise, it is merely a marvellous, fantastic, physical world, where everything resolves itself into material situations, sensuous enjoyments; infinitely picturesque and pleasant to the artistic sense, like a representation of some old eastern fairy tale on the stage: but in the modern world of actualities, the restless change and conflict, the perpetual hurrying onwards to the fulfilment of new destinies, new creeds, Hyderabad seems as utterly unreal, as detached, and illusive as a day dream....

You recollect those lines
'[illegible] renewed with its sighing
And Babylon itself in our midst' ....

(4)

Had the poet ever dreamed of this city he had substituted Hyderabad for Babylon...

Someday you must come here: and let me pay back in ever so slight a measure, the generous and delightful hospitality I received at your hands. Probably before then we two shall fly northward with the summer birds and claim a double measure of your kindness — the gods hasten that day!

Salaam alekum! Peace be on you O genial and gentle-hearted scholar dreaming in the benign shadow of your bronze Victory, and the poets' Hermes.

Your affectionate Indian god-child

Sarojini Naidu

Mrs Gosse is supposed to read a whole letter to herself between the lines of this.

(5)

whose wisdom was so immense, whose knowledge so limited!

Greek philosophy, all 'the glory that was Greece' was but the radiant flower that had the immemorial wisdom of the East for its roots: roots that sprang, were nurtured from the very core of eternal things.

Like Gautier, I am one for whom the visible world exists... this definite, dramatic world of so varied and fiery beauty, colour, music, perfume and vivid human faces. It is this deeply inherent instinct for a concrete and tangible world that effectually corrects and balances my eastern birth-right of mysticism, the ever-strengthening tendency and yearning to merge myself and become portion of the Abstract Universal Essence: Poets call it the Eternal Beauty, Philosophers the Ultimate Wisdom, Lovers the Immortal Love: and the rest name it God.

(6)

I carry your last words to me as a sort of talisman, a prophecy as well as a blessing. 'May you write beautiful poems.'

I have written nothing yet: but it is not you who will reproach me for my deliberate silence. I know of your letters to me, letters that I treasure, you describe me as an 'image of golden bronze' for the god to speak thro'.

Yes, I wait for the rare moment of ecstacy when the accents of the god are unmistakable. Many things vaguely stir in me, craving utterance. But I dare not speak till speech is inevitable and utters itself....

What an egoistical letter to send you! But why should not my literary sponsor be also father confessor of my literary faults?

There is no news of literary interest to send you of Hyderabad. There is no intellectual life here, no ardent, vital 'movement' ..... here and there, it is true, in some remote forest-dell or secluded hillside one might

Hyderabad Deccan
September 6th

Dear Mr Gosse,

Next to the delicacies of fine literature I know you love the delicacies of fine tobacco. I am sending you on your fift-third birthday a small cigarette case with a legend of the Great goddess Kali on the cover. In her four terrible hands she holds four separate blessings: Health, wealth, fame and happiness. How you would delight in a book I have been reading lately—an anthology of all the matchless ... Persian poetry. Some of them have delicious names (better than their verses): Scent of the jasmine, 'Rose bodied-heart's delight' 'Ornament of the World' (Yasman bi, Gulbadan, Dilshad, Jehanara)

Most of the ghazals and rubayats are full merely of an imitative sweetness—a flowing river of music rambling through gardens of conceits but one or two of the poetesses like the Empresses Nusfarat, the princess Zeb ul Nessa, daughter of Emperor Alamgir and Babi, write with a personal sincerity of rendition, fullness of music and freshness of literary magic. Impossible to render into English their lyrics are

Like poppies spread
You seize the flower the bloom is dead

Babi was a marvellous woman who in quite recent years founded a secret fanatic religious sect. She had an enormous following in Persia. The fierce ecstasy and occult beauty of her verses maddened them like new wine. She was imprisoned by the order of the late Shah and sentenced to death on account of her rapturous heresies, political and religious. There are thinking traditions connected with her name. Just before she was put to death, it is said stood like a prophetess in her cage. Such an implacable, exultant and defying connect of verse. For nearly two hours the multitudes stood spellbound and afraid. Her writing have been collected and are treasured with extreme secrecy by her followers.

Such women leaven the mediocrity of the world. After mentioning her naive logic, I am almost ashamed to send you my verses but you are as you have been all along my final literary court of appeal—you must pass sentence but pray don't discourage me! I am in the mood to work seriously. I have been evolving in my 'line unconsciousness' a hundred poems that must come to life sooner or later. ...

Yours Affectionately
Sarojini Naidu

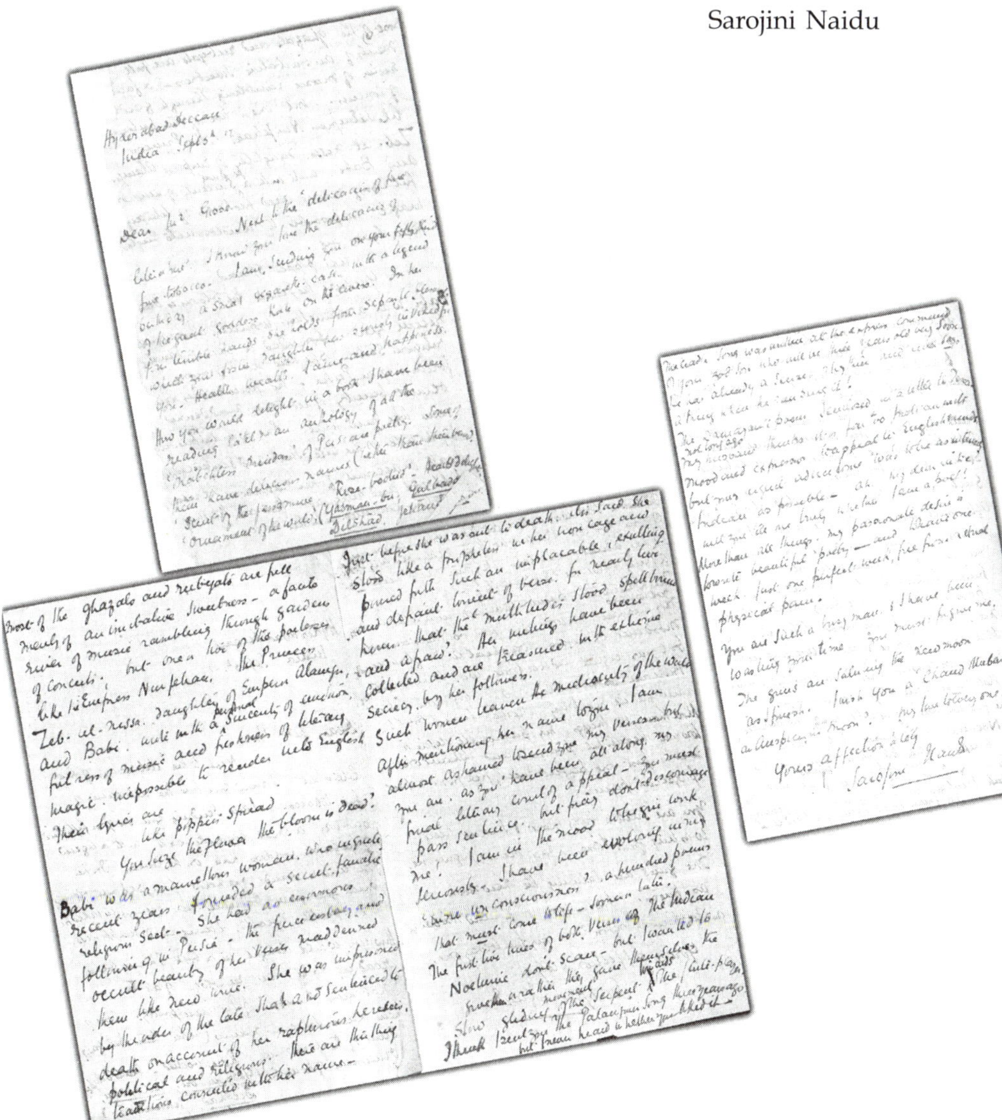

Hyderabad Deccan
24th December 1903

Dear Mr Gosse,

I am sending you for your severest criticism (I wish it could be praise) five little poems I wrote last week—the only poems of the year.

The first two verses of" Honey child" were there, as you know, seven years ago. The little "Henna" song pleases me very much because I didn't really write it. I merely transcribed the little kokila's song. Henna is an ornamental and national institution and it is customary for all girls and married women (but not widows) to stain their palms and fingernails with the bright red juice of henna leaves that symbolise gladness and festivity.

The "Ode to the Nizam" was presented two days ago, at the great Durbar held in honour of the Ramzan feast with a superb translation in Hindu verse by a well known Mohamedan poet. He took the plain robe of my English verse as it were, and embroidered it with all the gold and jewels of eastern eloquence and imagery. I should never dream of course of going fully unveiled in the midst of five hundred belted courtiers to the Nizam's court—it would be the scandal of India! As it is I suppose it is something novel in the annals of Indian tradition for a woman to present a poem to a sovereign in full durbar. It savours almost of the forbidden. The court of the Nizam is the only true eastern court left in India. It still upholds all the barbaric splendour that recalls the stories of the Arabian nights and I think among all the powers of India you cannot find a figure more picturesque more brilliant but alas more pathetic than the Nizam of Hyderabad. He affects all the dazzling caprices and follies of a potentiate with the real loneliness of a poet. Under happier circumstances of race and opportunity, he would have been a leader among men. But now he's merely the eastern Hamlet. His songs are exquisite and moving combining all the... mysticism of Cranshaw with the poignant human simplicity of Burns and the delicate art and melody of Tennyson. They are sung in all his four couplets alike by courtier and peasant, for they appeal equally to both. And at my wedding where my mother had a great reception for Mohemedan ladies, the women sang a beautiful selection of His Highness' ghazals.

I am sorry I have nothing better to send you than these little poems but I have been very ill throughout the year hardly ever leaving my bed for more than a week in two at a time. Next year if the gods will but permit me a few holidays from my perennial illness, I mean to recreate with all the golden bricks and mortar of verse of the dead leaders and legends, passionate to the beauties of the Nizam's dominions. Poet's have built Neneveh... and Babel itself in their "muth" and my... desires re build the antique glory of Hyderabad, Aurangabad, Gulberga and Warangal.

Please give my love to Mrs Gosse. To Tessa of the Rossetti hair and to the fair one with the 'gold luck', to Sylvia and to Lucifer my salutations.

May the New Year fulfil all your desires.

Your affectionate foster child,
Sarojini Naidu

24th December 1903.
Hyderabad Deccan.

Dear Mr Gosse.

I am sending you for your severest criticism (I wish it could be praise) five little poems I wrote last week – the only poems of the year. The first two verses of "Honey child" were written as you know, seven years ago. The little henna song pleases me very much, because I didn't really write it. I merely translated the little Kokila's song. "Henna" is an immemorial and national institution, and it is customary for all girls and married women (but not widows) to stain their palms and fingernails and feet with the bright red juice of henna leaves: it symbolises gladness and festivity.

The Ode to the Nizam was presented to him days ago at the great Durbar held in honour of the Ramzan Feast, with a superb translation in Urdu verse by a well known Mohomedan poet. He took the plain robe of my English verse and wove and embroidered it with all the gold and jewels of eastern eloquence and imagery. I should never dream, of course, of "singing faith unveiled" in the midst of five hundred belted courtiers to the Nizam's court – it would be the scandal of India. As it is, I suppose, it is something quite novel in the annals of Indian tradition for a woman to present a poem to a Sovereign in full durbar. It savours almost of the forbidden. The Court of the Nizam is the only true eastern court left in India. It still retains all the barbaric splendour that recalls the stories of the Arabian Nights. And I think among all the princes of India you cannot find

(3) a figure more picturesque more brilliant & alas more pathetic than the Nizam of Hyderabad. He affects all the dazzling caprices & follies of a potentate while the real loneliness of a poet: under happier circumstances of race and opulence he would have been a leader among men; but now he is merely the eastern Hamlet. His songs are exquisite and moving, combining all the fervid mysticism of Hafiz with the poignant human simplicity of Burns and the delicate art and melody of Tennyson – They are sung in all his four capitals, alike ~~[illegible]~~ by courtier & peasant for they appeal equally to both. And at my wedding when my mother had a great reception for Mohomedan ladies the singing women sang a beautiful selection of His Highness' *ghazals*. I am sorry I have nothing better to send you than these little poems but I have been

ill throughout the year, hardly ever leaving my bed for more than a week or two at a time. Next year, if the gods will but permit me a few holidays now & then from my "perennial illness" I mean to recreate with all the golden breaths & nectar of verse, the dead dramas and legends and passionate tales beauties of the Nizam's dominions. Poets have "built Nineveh with their sighing & Babel itself with their mirth", and my love and I will rebuild the antique glory of Hyderabad Aurangabad Gulbarga & Warangal –

Please give my love to Mrs Gosse, to Tessa of the Rossetti hair & to the fair one with the gold-locks "Sylphed" to Lucifer my salutations.

May the new year fulfil all your desires.

Your affectionate [illegible]
Sarojini Naidu

Hyderabad Deccan
5th May 1904

Dear Mr Gosse,

Will you forgive me if I claim half an hour of your very valuable time. I wish to ask your advice on a rather important subject. I am sending you 18 poems, five of which I think I sent you in January. But in case you did not receive them I have copied them out again with the others.

I sent this batch of poems some weeks ago to Arthur Symons and by the last mail I received a letter from him, a portion of which I copy for your consideration. He writes " you have never done anything so good as the best of these. They are filled with beauty captured at last. It no longer merely afloat in the air... I have no longer any doubt about you. You have a genuine note of your own in your verse. What you have written is fine and delicate... Now let me ask if you have enough poems as good as these you sent me to make a small volume? If so will you let me try to get it published and will you copy all the best verse you have and send it to me and allow me to choose out of it what I think would go best to make a book? I may get nobody to take it but I think I shall and I would like to write a preface to it if you would let me and add the drawing of you that Yeats' father did. ....All this is a sudden but a serious idea and I want you to consider it carefully and not to say no without a very good reason."

Of course I should not dream of saying yes without consulting you. It would be in my eyes an act of great disloyalty. You have been to me all these years, since I began to write at seventeen my 'literary godfather'. And now I know you will not grudge me the half hour I ask for to tell me very truly what you think of it all and whether these poems are really at last good enough to be given to the world. I think I have enough, with the few good poems you like from the old stock to make a little volume, but as I say I cannot think of bringing out a book without your hearty approval. If you wish a longer apprenticeship for me—well, I can wait; if not, shall I say yes to Arthur Symons?

There are one or two poems among these I am sending that I am very doubtful of like the "Indian Gipsy". And really all of them require finishing. They are just as I wrote them down in the first 'gush' of 'inspiration'!

I have a great many more in my head just now and I suppose they write themselves some day. I am of course absolutely at the mercy of my 'moods'. I cannot write when I wish and I dare not deny myself expression when the mood comes. This month I have been much stronger than normal; it is spring, rather half spring, half midsummer. If you can understand it, the heat is intense; but the trees are burgeoning all a glory of gold and purple and scarlet like a queen's garments.

May I expect to hear from you very soon? I send my love to Mrs Gosse, Tessa and Sylvia and of course to Lucifer.

I am yours affectionately
Sarojini Naidu

[illegible] May '04
Hyderabad Deccan.

Dear Mr Gosse. Will you forgive me if I claim half an hour of your very valuable time; I wish to ask your advice on a rather important subject.

I am sending you 18 poems five of which I think I sent you in January but in case you did not receive them I have copied them out again with the others.

I sent this batch of poems some weeks ago to Arthur Symons, and by the last mail I received a letter from him a portion of which I copy for your consideration. He writes: "You have never done anything so good as the best of these & they are filled with beauty captured at last, no longer merely afloat in the air .... I have no longer any doubt about you. You have a genuine note of your own in verse. What you have written is fine, firm and delicate .... Now let me ask if you have enough poems as good as these to make a small volume? If so will you let me try to get it published & will you copy all the best verse you have & send it to me & allow me to choose out of it what I think would go best to make a book? I may get nobody to take it but I think I shall. And I would like to write a preface but if you would let me, & add the drawing of you that Yeats' father did .... all this is a sudden but a serious idea, & I want you to consider it carefully & not to say no without very good reason" –

Of course I should not dream of saying yes without consulting you. It would be in my eyes an act of great disloyalty; you have been to me all these years, since I began to write at seventeen, my 'literary foster father'; and now I know you will not grudge me the half hour I ask for. It will be very kind, what you think of it all and whether these poems are really at last good enough to be given to the world. I think I have enough, with the few good poems you liked from the old stock to make a little volume; but as I say I would not think of bringing out a book without your approval. If you wish a longer apprenticeship for me – well, I can wait; if not shall I say yes to Arthur Symons?

There are one or two poems among these I am sending that I am very doubtful of – like the Indian Gypsy; and nearly all of them require finishing. They are just as I wrote them down in the first 'fresh' of 'inspiration'!!

I have a great many more in my head just now and I suppose they will write themselves some day. I am of course absolutely at the mercy of my 'moods'; I cannot write when I wish; & dare not deny myself expression when the mood comes.

This month I have been much stronger than usual; it is spring, or rather half spring, half midsummer. If you can understand it; the heat is intense; but the trees are burgeoning all a glory of gold and purple and scarlet like a queen's garments.

May I expect to hear from you very soon? I send my love to Mrs Gosse & Tessa & Sylvia & forgive [illegible] to decipher.

I am Yours affectionately
Sarojini Naidu.

Hyderabad
4th September 1905

Dear Mr Gosse,

My son your god child has written you an English letter all by himself for your birthday and he and I are sending you a little present—a copper vase of Cashmere. He wanted to fill it with sugar candy and raisins as he fancies his godfather's sweet tooth is as young as his for such delights—but I wish I could have filled it with long plumes of yellow mimosa that perfume this September month; or with sheaves of amber and red chrysanthemums, or with clusters of white roses and pink oleanders smelling of Paradise and beloved of the 'Great God'.

A happy birthday and as many more of them as go towards making a centenary. And for every year a new book as delightful as "French Profiles". Now isn't that an ideal wish? For you—for the public!

I am sending the few poems I have written this year—two or three of them were written early enough to be included in the "Golden Threshold", which by the way is at a standstill, I think. Some time ago I heard from Arthur Symons that Mr Heinemann would publish it and that an edition of 500 copies would cost 14 pounds—the binding extra. I at once wrote and asked him if I should send him 14 pounds immediately or wait till he let me know the total cost. And I have heard nothing since. Probably he is away. So I have made up my mind to write directly to Mr Heinemann and paid him 14 pounds this week so that there need be no delay in the printing. I am told that in India it will have a good "sale" but I don't care about sales much, nor the praises of a noted public. What I want is the approval of just a handful of people like you whose praise is for me real fame. It is just my 'horrid pride' as my husband says, but physically and mentally I shrink from the noise of crowds. Doubtless it is inherited from these immemorial ancestors of mine who sought shelter in the Himalayan caves and made friends with panthers! I wonder if you can realise how difficult it is for anyone to keep... to the primrose path of art in India.

France they say is the land of movements but Modern India I think is the "cradle & home ..."—There is a tacit understanding that all... should concentrate themselves on some practical end for the immediate and obvious good of the nation. There are innumerable strong foes who would lure you or face you with their non special work. The leader of a 'religious reform', the prophet of 'social progress', the edition of a political journal, the worker in the 'cause of female education' the president of a Home for Hindu widows, the advocate for the renewal of home industries—a whole paradox of admirable ... movements ... all people with scarcely enough bodily strength to exist at times and apart so unfitted to do more than sing with the birds in a forest of lilies and nut palms! And that is just what I have been doing not long ago—just singing with the birds in a wild and lonely garden set in a descent surrounded by hills, bare indeed of trees and blossoms but rich in ... legend. Such a garden full of wells decorated with friezes of fishes and buds and guarded by the ... living peacocks and fruit trees, groves of citron, orange, pomegranate and figs. Glowing flowers and free-falling fruit hanging together on the branches above running channels of green well water.

There's great excitement about the coming royal visit and at the moment my soul revels not on lyrics but clothes—as gorgeous as the verse of Mellon brocaded with gold and silver on phlox red and iris purple silks and delicate and diaphanous as the lyrics of Shelly. All floating gauzes edged with silver, fringe and pearls. Coloured like the petals of rose and the heart of a Kanak Champa—can you imagine anything more eastern and more purposeless—as to the sound of the 'Verbal vision'. Things are always a little more sober, a little less magnificent when translated into actual fabrics. It is a little parable of the supremity of actual life, isn't it?

I am writing a great deal of nonsense—and I know time with you is like opals. So let me first add my affectionate... messages for Mrs Gosse, Tessa... Sylvia of the Gold—locks, Philip and Lucifer prince of cats—and Margaret who thinks you are the cleverest man in the world.

I long to see you all again and have portraits of you and the new house. I am getting aged—actually 26 years old! And my body is bent with the cares of motherhood—such children! Imps and elves and angels all in one, but my heart, my heart remains always the loving heart of the old Sarojini.

Believe me Yours Affectionately
Sarojini Naidu

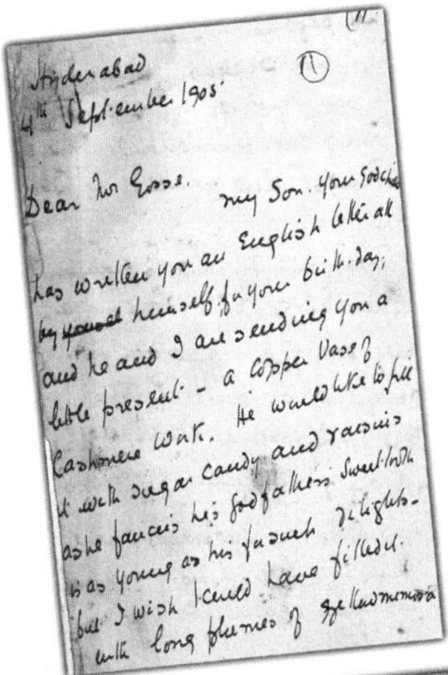

Hyderabad
4th September 1905 (1)

Dear Mr Gosse.
my Son. Your Godchild
has written you an English letter all
by himself for your birthday;
and he said I am sending you a
little present – a Copper Vase of
Cashmere Work. He would like to fill
it with sugar candy and raisins
as he fancies his godfather's sweet tooth
is as young as his youthful delights –
but I wish I could have filled it
with long plumes of yellow mimosa

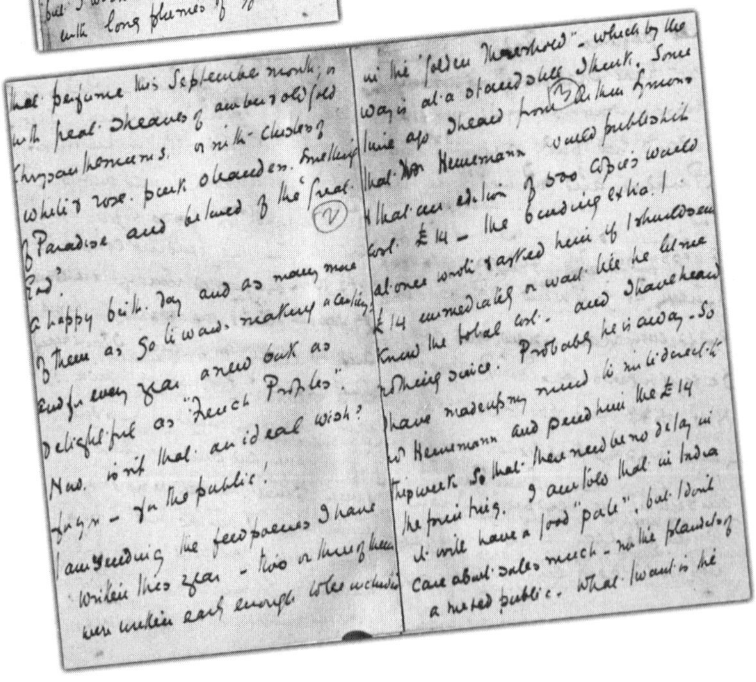

that perfume this September month; or
with pearl sheaves of amber and gold
chrysanthemums. or with clusters of
white rose. pink oleander. smelling
of Paradise and beloved of the 'Great
God'. (2)
A happy birthday and as many more
of them as Solomon's. making a [illegible]
and for every year a new book as
delightful as "French Profiles".
Now. is it not an ideal wish?
[illegible] – for the public!
I am sending the few poems I have
written this year – two or three of them
were written early enough to be included

in the 'Golden Threshold' – which by the
way is at a standstill I think. Some
time ago I heard from (3) [illegible]
that Mr Heinemann would publish it
& that an edition of 500 copies would
cost £14 – the binding extra. I
at once wrote & asked him if I should send
£14 immediately or wait till he let me
know the total cost. and I have heard
nothing since. Probably he is away – so I
have made up my mind to write direct to
Mr Heinemann and send him the £14
this week so that there need be no delay in
the printing. I am told that in India
it will have a good "sale", but I don't
care about sales much – nor the plaudits of
a mixed public. What I want is the

(4)

pproval of just a handful of people who
n – whose praise is fame – real fame;
it is just my 'lurid pride' as my husband
says. but physically & mentally I shrink from
the noise of crowds. Doubtless it is inherited
from those immemorial ancestors of mine
who sought shelter in the Himalayan caves
and contemplation and made friends with
panthers!

I wonder if you can realize how difficult
it is for any one to keep 'merely' to the
'primrose path' of Art – in India
France they say is the land of movements;
but Modern India I think the cradle
& home & hair bin" – There is always a lack
understanding that all talents and
enthusiasms should concentrate themselves

(5)

on some practical end for the immediate
and obvious good of the nation. There are
innumerable strong forces who would lure
you or face you with their noisy special
work. The leader of a 'religious reform' the
prophet of 'social progress' the editor of a
political journal. the worker in the
cause of 'female education' the president
of a Home for Hindu Widows'. the advocate
for the revival of home industries – a
whole paradox of admirable and inconfirm
movements whose pressed on home – home
of all people. with scarcely enough
bodily strength to exist at times – &
a pure so unfitted to do more than

(6)

ing with the birds in a forest of lilies
and nut palms! And. that is just what
have been doing not long ago – just
singing with the birds in a wild & lonely
garden set in a desert. bounded by
hills. bare indeed of trees & blossom
but within its inner legend – such a
garden full of wells decorated with
friezes of fishes & birds. & guarded by
lions & living peacocks – and fruit-trees
groves of citron. orange. pomegranate
and figs. glowing flowers and
fragrant fruit hanging together
on the branches above running
channels of green well water.

There is great excitement about the
coming royal visit and at the moment
myself resolved for lyrics but clothes –
as gorgeous as the very mellow brocades
with gold & silver on purple. red and rich purple
silks; as delicate and diaphanous as the
lyrics of Shelley. all floating gauzes
edged with silver fringe & pearls. coloured
like the petals of rose and and the heart of
a Kanak. Champa – Can you imagine
anything more eastern & more sumptuous –
as to the sound of all the 'verbal visions' things
are always a little more sober. a little
less magnificent when translated into
actual fabrics. It is a little parable of
the superiority of Art over life – isn't it?

I am writing a great deal of nonsense –
and I know time with you. is like gold –
So let me just add my affectionate
influences and messages for Louis Jones.
Dessa of the delicate hair. Sylvia of the
Goldilocks. Philip and Lucifer
Prince of Cats – & Margaret who
thinks you are the cleverest man in
the world. I long to see you all again
and have portraits of you & the new horizon
I am getting aged. actually 26 years old.
and my body is bent – with the cares of
motherhood – such children! imps & elves
and angels all in one – but my heart. my
heart remains always the loving heart
of the old Sarojini –

Hyderabad Deccan
12th January 1906

Dear Mr Gosse,

Your very kind letter gave me great pleasure but I did not answer it immediately as I wished to consider the question of publication very carefully before giving my decided reply.

Before I proceed further let me assure you that if you consider it advisable to publish under the conditions you mention in your letter, there will be no difficulty in meeting my share of the 'risks' whenever necessary, if you can give me an approximate idea of the amount. I wish to write to you very frankly about my own feelings in the matter.

Living in Hyderabad, the most self-centred of all Indian principalities, absolutely isolated from all living literary influences and a public, my personal ambition for success for fame has been growing less and less. Though of course the passionate longing to produce art is part of myself and cannot be quelled. When Arthur Symons wrote to me proposing that I should seriously consider collecting my verses into a little book I was not too eager to fall in with his plan. Though I value his opinion immensely, my husband who strongly disapproves of my growing indifference to publicity, practically forced me to give my consent, subject of course to your favourable opinion. Then when a few weeks ago your letter came announcing the failure of Mr Grant Richards and the consequent difficulty in finding another publisher to take my manuscript, will you believe me if I say I was almost relieved and probably I should have let the matter drop there if you had not so kindly suggested and advised an alternative backed by your most precious and inspiring personal sympathy and interest.

Almost directly after receiving your letter we went to Bombay for the Great Annual National Congress Conference meetings where the acknowledged leaders of modern Indian thought and progress were gathered together from all parts of the country. To my great amazement, it was nothing less—so far from being the insignificant little provincial I had thought myself, I was treated almost as a national possession. I! And I had my share of the ovations accorded to the 'lions' of the day.... It was doubtless an exaggerated kindness, partly it was that I appealed to their sense of Chivalry. As I have not yet my lack of dignity and national purpose, but it was a great awakening for me, changing in a moment all my sense of proportion—of responsibility or rather irresponsibility.

I realised fully for the first time that 'no man liveth with himself', especially one to whom any gift however small has been entrusted... It was not a moment of pride so much as of humiliation... The public was waiting for me—no, not for me, so much as for a poet, a national poet and it was ready to accept me if I would only let it—I would be a little true to my own power and realise the polemic of all act for good and evil..... This wholly undeserved tribute from the great Indian public—the loving, thanking public outside my sleepbound little city of Hyderabad finally decided me to say 'yes' to your suggestion.

You will understand that I am writing to you as I feel and not through any vanity or conceit. I do not for a single moment imagine that what I have written possesses any abiding charm and beauty but I do not honestly hope and believe that someday if my very precarious health permits me sufficient years I shall indeed produce something worthy to be offered to my nation as a gift. Something worthy of the great kindness you have shown me all these years discloses with your prophetic sympathy the folded possibilities that lie within me, in spite of all the worthless and mediocre results of my earlier attempts at writing.

I am sending a fresh manuscript to be used instead of the one I sent Arthur Symons. In this one I have included three or four new poems and omitted one or two of the earlier ones. If you could spare the time I should be glad of any further omissions you might care to make. I have not quite settled on a title for the book. I send a few for you to choose from. May I mention incidentally that I must have a very beautiful get up - simple but beautiful to satisfy my childish love for exquisite 'superficials'. I have not included the dedication, as I wish to send it later when everything has been satisfactorily arranged.

I am behaving like a real god-daughter, laying so much responsibility and trouble on my God-father's shoulders, but remember you were really the very first who helped and encouraged me to write—to add my little exotic flower to the glorious garland of English verse.

I must not take up a single moment more of your time except to wish you and Mrs. Gosse and the girls a very happy new year, rich with every bit of blessing and prosperity. To Lucifer, son of the Morning, I send my salutations.

Believe me Yours affectionately
Sarojini Naidu

I think Mrs Gosse will be pleased to hear that I am becoming a famous housekeeper. And that I am a great authority on cauliflowers and peas! I wish I could send her a hamper from my kitchen garden with a hundred or so of my roses and carnations, all your English flowers growing out in the open in Indian January.

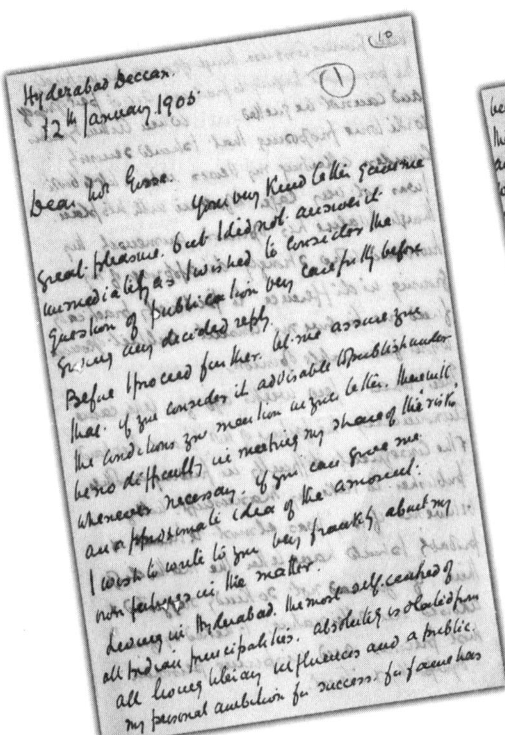

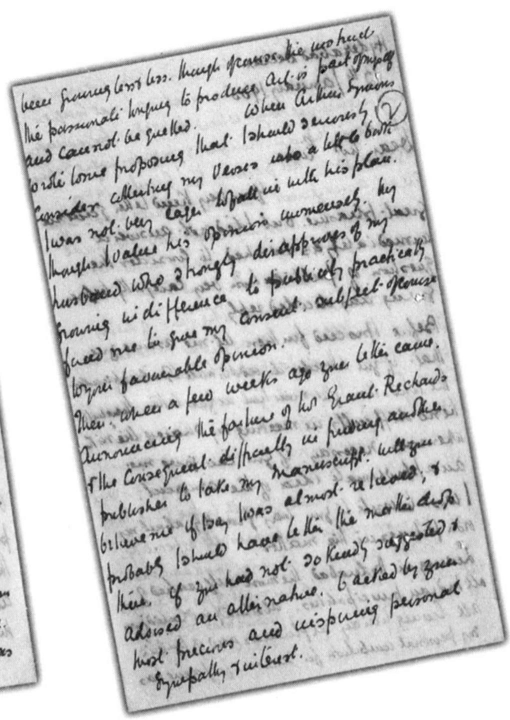

Almost directly after receiving your letter, we went to Bombay, for the great Annual National Congress & Conference meetings, where the acknowledged leaders of modern Indian thought & progress were gathered together from all parts of the Country. To my (3) great amazement – it was rather hard – so far from being the insignificant little provincial I had thought myself, I was treated almost as a national possession – I! and I had my share of the ovations accorded to the 'lions' of the day... It was doubtless an exaggerated kindness, partly it was that I appealed to their sense of Chivalry, as I am not yet outgrown my lack of dignity and natural petulance – but it was a great awakening for me. Changing in a moment all my sense of proportion – of responsibility & irresponsibility. I realized fully for the first time that "no man liveth unto himself" especially one to whom any gift, however small, has been entrusted.... It was not a moment of pride so much as of humiliation ... my public was waiting for me – no, not for me, so much as for a poet, a national poet, and it was ready to accept me

if I would only let it – if I would be a little true to my own powers and realize the potency of all art for good & evil. This was right, & wholly understood too, but from the great Indian public – the loving, thinking public, outside my sleepy old little city of Hyderabad – finally decided me to [illegible] 'Yes' to your suggestion.

You will understand that I am writing to you as I feel – and not through any vanity or conceit. I do not for a single moment imagine that what I have written possesses any abiding charm or beauty; but I do honestly hope and believe that someday, if my very precarious health permits me sufficient years, I shall indeed produce something worthy to be offered to you, not as a gift – something worthy of the great kindness you have shown me all these years, & discerning, with your prophetic sympathy, the folded possibilities that lie within me, in spite of all my worthless and mediocre results of my earlier attempts at writing —

I am sending a fresh manuscript which I used (5) instead of the one I sent Arthur Symons. In this one I have included three or four new poems, & omitted one or two of the earlier ones. If you could spare the time I should be glad of any further omissions you might care to make.

I have not quite settled on a title for the book. I send a few for you to choose from. May I mention incidentally that I must have a very beautiful 'get-up' – simple, but really beautiful, to satisfy my childish love of exquisite "superficials".

I have not included the dedication, as I wish to send it later, when everything has been satisfactorily arranged.

I am behaving like a real god daughter – laying so much responsibility and trouble on my god father's shoulders; but, remember, you were really the very first who helped & encouraged me to write – to add my little exotic flower to the glorious garland of English verse –

must not take up a single moment more of your time, except to wish you and Mrs Gosse and the girls a very happy new year – rich with every sort of blessing & prosperity. To Lucifer, Son of the Morning, I send my Salutations.

Believe me. Yours affectionately

Sarojini Naidu

I think Mrs Gosse will be pleased to hear that I am becoming a famous housekeeper, and that I am a great authority on cauliflowers and marrowfat peas! I wish I could send her a hamper from my kitchen garden [illegible] with a hundred or so of my roses and carnations & all your English flowers growing out in the open in our Indian January –

Hyderabad Deccan
14th July 1911

Dear Godfather of my lyrical girlhood –

For the sake of the timid girl of long ago, will you spare me an hour to read these few poems of my "middle age"? I feel more timid and far more in need of your encouragement and praise and candour than ever in those far off days when I was seventeen and life went gaily for me "like a laugh from the lips of a dream" and "like a tear from the eyes of a bride" combined.

I fear the singing note you used to praise has almost died out of my verses now. But I feel that perhaps a graver note has crept in since I have lived in such close comradeship with the sorrow of human hearts. Will you tell me... if these verses have any real value? I have just written them down as they came to me and they all want revising. The labour of the file. Sometimes I think two or three of them good— "The Dirge", the song that begins may say the world is full of fear and hate and perhaps the sonnet "Death stroked my hand". As for the rest, I can't judge if they are poetry at all but I know that they were all written in utter sincerity in accordance with the moments, moods and the moods' conflicts with one another. How can I help the inconsistency that is part of my temperament? I am sending you these verses now because Mr Heinemann who has seen some of them seems very anxious to bring them out in book form. He thinks some of them "fine English poetry" and says they are sure of a cordial reception; that these new poems are a great step forward in every way from the Golden Threshold. He is such a fine critic that I cannot of course doubt his judgement but unless *you* give me a favourable verdict I cannot summon the courage to publish them in a book! It is very strange that I who am perhaps by nature and cut out by circumstances quite fearless in facing most things absolute humbly when it comes to a question of my own verses—my ideal is so high and alas my accomplishments so feeble so capricious, so wholly disappointing to me.

However if you say that they are good I shall believe they are good and give them to Mr Heinemann to publish when he likes. Either before or after the Durbar as seems most advisable from the publisher's point of view. If before–the book will be very tiny of about 25 to 30 poems; if after, there may be a few more. I have only been able to copy out 14 which are under separate registered post. Next week I'll send you some of the others. I do feel somewhat remorseful of giving you so much trouble because of my illegible handwriting, but I think if the poetry is good you will pardon that. If the poetry is bad—well... This is a most dull and horrid letter I am writing to catch the mail!

I was very nearly on the point of seeing you last year—you and my dear Mrs Gosse and Tessa and dear Arthur Symons and all my friends. I was very ill and I was hastily being packed off to the hospital for an operation. But somehow I got patched up again for a little while and though one has to adjust one's life to continuous pain; it is a wonderful thing to feel that sometimes one is a little better. I am, as someone said, always at the point of death or in deliverance from death! But that is an exaggeration. It is nothing so exciting or dramatic as that but I cannot pretend that my bad health does not handicap me with all my work to do—that *must* be done! So one just takes one's bodily suffering in one's hand and lays it on the alter together with all one's gifts of love and services...

Sometimes I do rebel that I have not the ... atmosphere to write nice poetry but then I feel that to me dreams and deeds, song and service are the compliments of each other and are indeed interchangeable. And if at the moment the service is more urgently needed than the song, why, who am I that I should question? The great thing is to give all of oneself in a lyric silence in a time of action. As well as a lyric song in a time of rest. I think you will understand and not misjudge me when I speak like this. To whom should I say this if not to you, who hoped that I was going to be a great poet. I do not know if the day will ever come when I shall write a really great and beautiful poem. I be as once you said a Keats and a Goethe to India. But while I live it will always be the supreme desire of my soul to write poetry—one poem, one line of enduring verse even. Perhaps I shall die without realising that longing which is at once an exquisite joy and unspeakable anguish to me—who knows? And yet, and yet. I know in every fibre of me that I am a poet.

My children are growing up very fast, body and spirit. It is a great joke against me that I look so absolutely small to be their mother. And they too quite appreciate the joke and say I am a "changeling mother", not a very useful scolding mother at all but a sort of "fairy tale Godmother" mother who does nothing but make poems. Such foolish poems, says my little girl in her crisp contemplation of English, all about things that never happened and people she never saw—but all the same

My husband is going ... to the Delhi Durbar but I am not sure if I am going ... But I dare say in the end I shall go and wear more sumptuous clothes. "Shot opal gold and amethyst" and then I shall buy or design myself a pair of new earrings for the occasion. Shall they be turquoise to match the sky or chrysoprase to reveal the sea? Or of opal to interpret ... the changing dreams of my soul?

Give my love to Mrs Gosse and Tessa and Philip and Mrs Philip & baby Philip and to pretty Sylvia. I hear Maurice ... has become a poet ... What is Robbie Ross doing and how is Arthur Waugh? Can you tell me anything of Arthur Symons. It breaks my heart to think of him.

Yours Affectionately
Sarojini Naidu

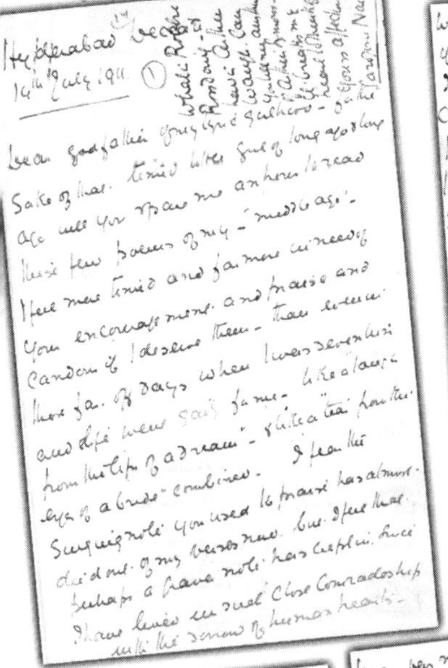

Hyderabad Deccan
14th July 1911

(1)

Dear godfather of my lyric girlhood — for the sake of that timid little girl of long ago & long ago will you spare me an hour to read these few poems of my "middle age". I feel more timid and far more in need of your encouragement and praise and candour if I deserve them — than even in those far off days when I was seventeen and life was "sadly fine — like a laugh from the lips of a dream — & like a tear from the eyes of a bride" combined. I fear the surprising note you used to praise has almost died out of my verses now. But I feel that perhaps a graver note has crept in since I have lived in such close comradeship with the sorrow of human hearts —

What is Robbie Ross doing? — the last I heard. Can you tell him why I have heard nothing of him & it breaks my heart to think [illegible]. Yours affectionately Sarojini Naidu

(2)

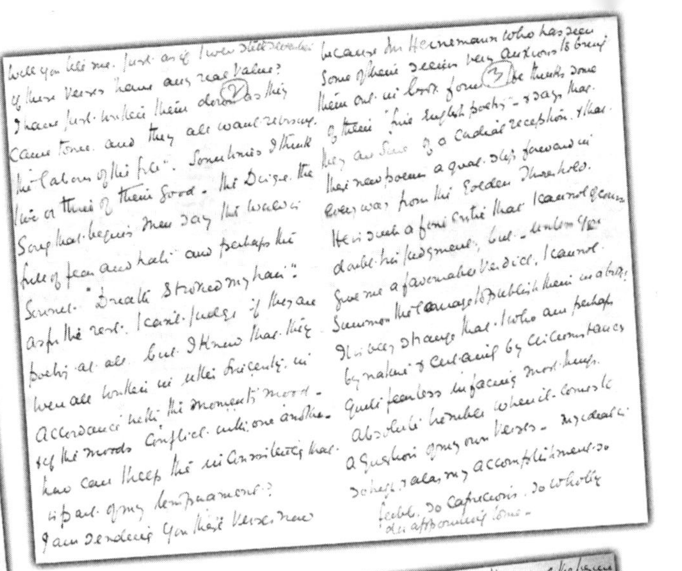

Will you tell me, just as if I were still seventeen, if these verses have any real value? I have just written them down as they came to me and they all want revising. "The labour of the file." Sometimes I think two or three of them good. The Dirge. The Song that begins "New day the [illegible]" full of fear and hate and perhaps the sonnet "Death strokes my hair". As for the rest, I can't judge if they are poetry at all. But I know that they were all written in utter sincerity in accordance with the moment's mood — & if the moods conflict with one another how can I help the inconsistency that is part of my temperament? I am sending you these verses now

(3)

because Mr Heinemann who has seen some of them seems very anxious to bring them out in book form. He thinks some of them "fine English poetry" & says that they are sure of a cordial reception & that these new poems are a great step forward in every way from the Golden Threshold. He is such a fine critic that I cannot of course doubt his judgement, but unless you give me a favourable verdict, I cannot summon the courage to publish them in a book. It is very strange that I who am perhaps by nature & certainly by circumstances quite fearless in facing most things, am absolutely a coward when it comes to a question of my own verses — my dearest & alas my accomplishment so scrappy, so capricious, so wholly feeble, so disappointing [illegible] —

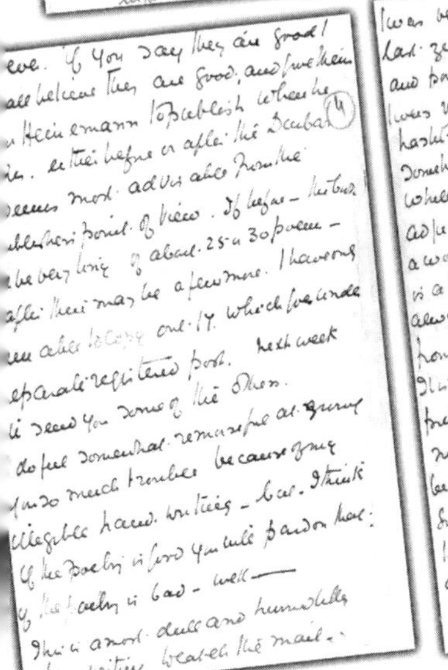

(4)

ever. If you say they are good I shall believe they are good, and give them to Heinemann to publish whether [illegible] either before or after the Durbar. It seems most advisable from the publisher's point of view. If before — the book will be very tiny of about 25 or 30 poems — after there may be a few more. I have only been able to copy out 17 which I will send under separate registered post. Next week I'll send you some of the others. I do feel somewhat remorseful at giving you so much trouble because of my illegible hand-writing — but I think if the poetry is good you will pardon that; if the poetry is bad — well — This is a most dull and horrid letter I am writing to catch the mail.

(5)

I was very nearly on the point of seeing you last year. You and my dear Mrs Gosse & Tessa and poor dear Arthur Symons & all my friends — I was very, very ill and I was going to be packed off for an operation but somehow I got patched up again for a little while, and though of course one has to adjust one's life to continual pain, sometimes one [illegible] a wonderful thing to feel that — I am as someone said [illegible] is a whole being! — always at the point of death or of [illegible] from death! But that is an exaggeration — it is nothing so exciting or dramatic as that — but I cannot pretend that my bad health does not handicap me with all my work to do — that must be done. So one just has to take one's body's suffering in one's hand and lay it on the altar together with all one's gifts of love and service — a thorny flame indeed, but not the less acceptable to Him for whose dear sake a dreamer of dreams has grown to a doer of deeds —

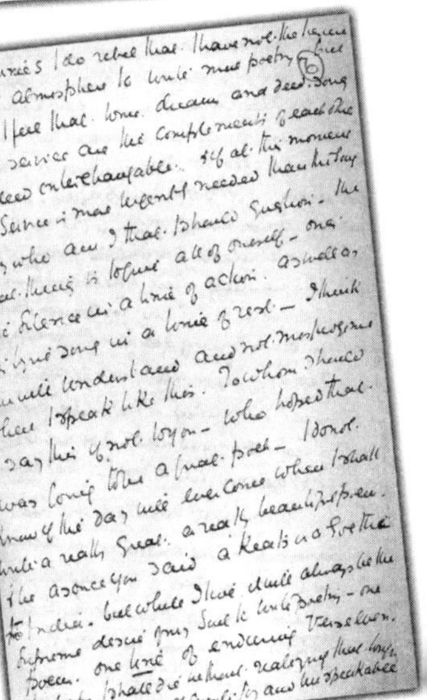

(6)

Sometimes I do rebel that I have not the leisure or the atmosphere to write more poetry but then I feel that love, dream and deed, song and service are the complements of each other & indeed interchangeable, & if at this moment the service is more urgently needed than the song why who am I that I should question. The great thing is to give all of oneself — one's silence in a time of action as well as one's lyric song in a time of rest. — I think you will understand and not misinterpret when I speak like this. To whom should I say this if not to you — who hoped that I was going to be a great poet — I do not know if the day will ever come when I shall write a really great, a really beautiful poem. The poem you said a Keats or a Goethe for India — but while I live it will always be the supreme desire of my soul to write poetry — one line of enduring verse, poem. One line of enduring [illegible] — perhaps I shall die without realising that longing which is at once an exquisite joy and an unspeakable

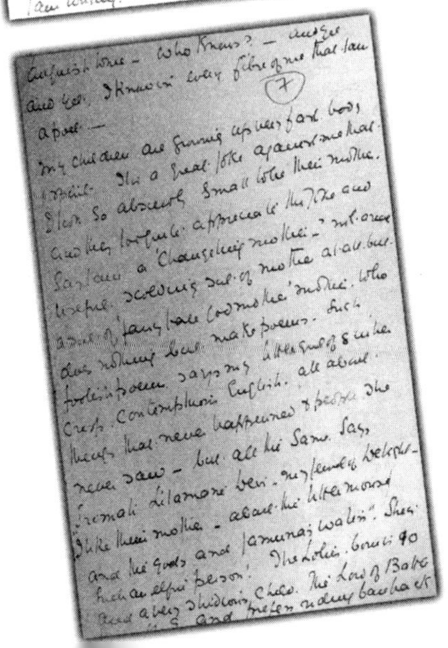

(7)

anguish too — who knows? — and yet I know in every fibre of me that I am a poet —

My children are growing up very fast — boys and girls. It is a great joke against me that I look so absurdly small like their mother. And they love to appreciate the joke and [illegible] a "changeling mother" not a [illegible] scolding sort of mother at all but useful, a sort of fairy tale godmother who does nothing but make poems. Such foolish poems, says my little girl of 8 in her crisp contemptuous English, all about things that never happened & people she never saw — but all the same, says [illegible] Lilamani [illegible] — about the little mouse like their mother — about the gods and Jamuna's waters. She is such an elfin person! The Lotus, born in 90 [illegible] a very [illegible] child. The Lord of [illegible] and [illegible]

(8)

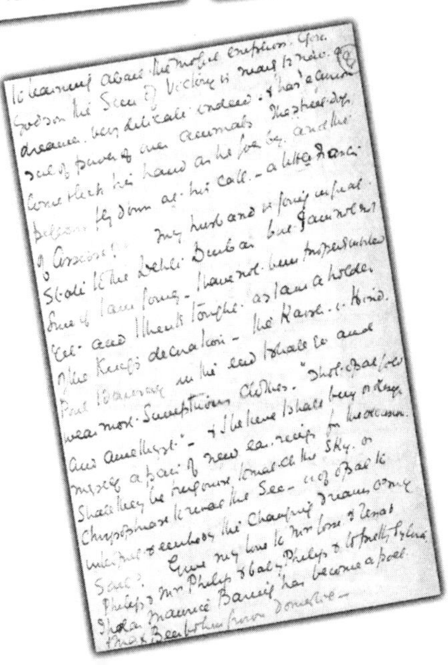

to learning about the noble creation. [illegible] God on the seen of Victory is ready to [illegible] & has a [illegible] dreamer, very delicate indeed, & has the strange power over animals. The sheep & dogs come & lick his hand as he goes by, and the pigeons fly down at his call — a little St Francis of Assisi! My husband is going up to the Delhi Durbar — but I am not sure if I am going. I have not been [illegible] tell and I think tonight, as I am a holder of the King's decoration — the Kaiser-i-Hind. In the end I shall go and wear most sumptuous clothes. "Shot of [illegible] and amethyst" — & I believe I shall beg or [illegible] myself a pair of new earrings for the occasion. Shall they be turquoise to match the sky or chrysoprase to match the sea — or opal to whisper & echo the changing dreams of my soul? Give my love to Mrs Gosse & Tessa & Philip & Mrs Philip & baby Philip & to pretty Sylvia. Is that Maurice Baring has become a poet. Max Beerbohm [illegible] —